New International Business English

Communication skills in English for business purposes

Workbook

Leo Jones
Richard Alexander

CAMBRIDGE
UNIVERSITY PRESS

PUBLISHED BY THE PRESS SYNDICATE OF THE UNIVERSITY OF CAMBRIDGE
The Pitt Building, Trumpington Street, Cambridge, United Kingdom

CAMBRIDGE UNIVERSITY PRESS
The Edinburgh Building, Cambridge CB2 2RU, UK   http://www.cup.cam.ac.uk
40 West 20th Street, New York, NY 10011–4211, USA   http://www.cup.org
10 Stamford Road, Oakleigh, Melbourne 3166, Australia

First published 1989
New edition 1996
Reprinted 1999

Printed in the United Kingdom at the University Press, Cambridge

A catalogue record for this book is available from the British Library

ISBN 0 521 45579 0 Workbook
ISBN 0 521 45578 2 Workbook Cassette Set
ISBN 0 521 45580 4 Student's Book
ISBN 0 521 45577 4 Student's Book Cassette Set
ISBN 0 521 45576 6 Teacher's Book
ISBN 0 521 42735 5 Video Teacher's Guide
ISBN 0 521 42732 0 Video Cassette (VHS PAL)
ISBN 0 521 42733 9 Video Cassette (VHS SECAM)
ISBN 0 521 42734 7 Video Cassette (VHS NTSC)

Contents

Introduction

What does the Workbook contain?

Background information: Information to help you to deal with the activities in the Student's Book for this unit.

Functions: Extra practice in using useful expressions presented in the Student's Book – some of these are Speaking exercises included on the Workbook recordings.

Vocabulary: Revision of vocabulary presented in the activities and texts in the Student's Book.

Prepositions (in Units 5 to 15): Exercises on prepositions and prepositional phrases.

Word-building (in Units 5, 7, 9, 11, 13 and 15): Exercises on using prefixes and suffixes to form compound words.

Listening: Practice in understanding interviews, broadcasts and discussions on business topics – there are also note-taking tasks based on recorded messages on the Workbook recordings.

Writing: Short writing tasks with model versions in the Answer Key.

Reading: Practice in understanding reading texts on business topics.

Grammar review: Revision of the main 'problem areas' of English grammar.

And at the back of the book:

The Answer Key: Answers or Suggested answers to the exercises and model versions of the Writing tasks.

Transcripts: Transcripts of the Listening exercises.

What's on the Workbook recordings?

The two Workbook recordings contain the Listening exercises and Speaking exercises. Full instructions on what to do are given in the Workbook itself.

The Listening exercises usually consist of several tasks and you'll need to listen to the recording more than once. If you're using a cassette player with a counter, make sure you set it to ZERO at the start of each exercise, so that you can easily find the beginning again. The text of these recordings is included in the Transcripts at the back of the book – you should not look at these until AFTER you've tried doing the task and checked your answers in the Answer Key.

In the Speaking exercises you'll need to 'talk to the people in the recording', but there's usually no need to record your own voice. If you do want to record your own voice, you'll need to use a blank cassette. The Speaking exercises give practice in using useful functional expressions and they will help you to develop your fluency.

How do I use the Workbook and the Answer Key?

The Background information sections are designed to give you more information about the theme of the unit. If you don't have much experience of the business world, you should study these sections before the class begins work on the unit.

The Vocabulary, Grammar review, Prepositions, Word-building, Listening and Reading exercises are related to the theme of the Student's Book unit, but not directly to any particular section in the unit.

The Functions exercises contain follow-up work on language points that are presented in the Student's Book. You'll usually find it easier to do these Workbook exercises after you've done the equivalent sections in the Student's Book.

The Answer Key contains answers to all the exercises. For some exercises, the answers we give are 'Suggested answers': this means that variations are often possible which are equally correct. If you don't understand why some of your answers are wrong or different from the model answers given, you may need to ask your teacher about this.

If possible, try to refer to the Answer Key AFTER you've tried each exercise. You'll find that you'll learn better by looking at the answers later – and that the exercises are more enjoyable if you have to think hard about them.

With the Writing tasks, once you have compared your work with the model version in the Key, you may need to ask your teacher to look at your work and show you where you have made any mistakes in grammar, spelling or punctuation.

Should I do *all* the exercises in the Workbook?

No. Your time is probably limited and certainly precious, so you'll need to *select* which exercises to do in the Workbook. You'll need to decide which of the exercises will be most useful and interesting for you, bearing in mind what you have done in class for each unit. If necessary, ask your teacher for advice on which exercises to do.

As a general rule, if you've found a particular language point *easy* in class, don't do the equivalent exercise in the Workbook. If you find a particular skill *difficult*, you should spend time on developing this skill using the Workbook exercises – for example, if you find it hard to understand people speaking English at a natural speed, you should spend plenty of time doing the Listening exercises using the Workbook recordings.

What else can I do on my own?

Reading, listening and speaking: As well as working through this Workbook, try to seek opportunities to read, listen to and speak English in other ways. Maybe subscribe to a weekly English-language newspaper or magazine, such as *The Economist*. If possible, listen to radio programmes in English, such as the BBC World Service or the Voice of America (VOA). If you have access to them, watch English-language satellite TV programmes, or go to the cinema or watch videos to see films in the original English version. And, of course, take any opportunities of speaking English to people – visitors to your company or language institute, tourists, friends of friends, etc.

Preparation for class work: You can save time in class by preparing the sections in the Student's Book which you'll be doing in class – read them through and look up any unfamiliar words.

After class: You can help yourself to remember by reading through the sections you did in class again. Look back through the pages you've done and notice the words and phrases you've highlighted – this will help you to memorize and revise the vocabulary.

Vocabulary: Highlight new words in the Student's Book, in the Workbook and in magazines or newspapers. Use a pocket-size notebook to write down new, useful vocabulary and expressions. Writing things down is a good way of helping yourself to memorize words and an easy way of finding them again later when you need to refresh your memory.

If you come across an unfamiliar word (like *precious* in the first line of the previous section – and not just 'Business English words'), you should look it up in an English-to-English dictionary. Look carefully at the examples given in the dictionary, not just the definition, and – if you think it will be useful in future – write the word down in your vocabulary notebook.

We recommend that you invest in an English-to-English learner's dictionary – ask your teacher to suggest a good one.

Good luck!

Leo Jones   Richard Alexander

1 Face to face

1.1 Dealing with people   *Background information*

These 'Background information' sections will be particularly useful if you don't have practical experience of working in business, or if you don't have personal experience of the theme of a particular unit. If you've been working in business for some time, we suggest that you read these sections quickly through to revise some of the vocabulary and the ideas.

In business, people have to deal in person with all kinds of people. You may have to use English when talking to different people within your company who don't speak your language: these may be colleagues or co-workers, superiors or subordinates – who may work with you in your own department, in another part of the building or in another branch. And you may also have to deal in English with people from outside the organization: clients, suppliers, visitors and members of the public. Moreover, these people may be friends, acquaintances or strangers – people of your own age, or people who are younger or older than you. The relationship you have with a person determines the kind of language you use.

This relationship may even affect what you say when you meet people: for example, it's not appropriate to say '*Hi, how are you!*' when meeting the Managing Director of a large company or to say '*Good morning, it's a great pleasure to meet you*' when being introduced to a person you'll be working closely with in the same team.

Remember that people form an impression of you from the way you speak and behave – not just from the way you do your work. People in different countries have different ideas of what sounds friendly, polite or sincere – and of what sounds rude or unfriendly! Good manners in your culture may be considered bad manners in another.

Remember also that your body language, gestures and expression may tell people more about you than the words you use.

Each of these sentences has a nationality word missing. Add the missing words to the puzzle. Remember to use a Capital Letter. (The first one is done for you as an example.)

1 If he comes from Cairo, he must be ....
2 If she lives in Paris, she must be ....
3 If they live in Brussels, my guess is that they're ....
4 If he lives in Warsaw, I expect he's ....
5 If she comes from Rome, she's ...., I suppose.
6 He works in Tokyo, so I think he's ....
7 As she's from Budapest, I presume she's ....
8 If he comes from Toronto, he probably speaks ....
9 If they live in São Paulo, they're probably ....
10 As they live in Athens, I think they're ....
11 He lives in Beijing, so presumably he's ....
12 Her home town is Amsterdam, so I guess she's ....
13 Their head office is in Madrid: they are a .... firm.
14 If they work in Kuala Lumpur, I expect they're ....
15 He has a house in Istanbul, so he must be ....
16 If they come from Edinburgh and Cardiff, they're both ....

8 | E g y p t i a n

1.3 Go along and get along *Reading*

Read this article and then answer the questions that follow:

Go along and get along

THE Japan Society's crash course on how to bridge the chasm between Japanese and American managers forces participants to examine their own cultural assumptions, as well as to learn about the other side. Behaviour which Americans consider trustworthy is often precisely that which Japanese associate with shifty characters – and vice versa.

To Americans, people who pause before replying to a question are probably dissembling. They expect a trustworthy person to respond directly. The Japanese distrust such fluency. They are impressed by somebody who gives careful thought to a question before making a reply. Most Japanese are comfortable with periods of silence. Americans find silence awkward and like to plug any conversational gaps.

The cherished American characteristics of frankness and openness are also misunderstood. The Japanese think it is sensible, as well as polite, for a person to be discreet until he is sure that a business acquaintance will keep sensitive information confidential. An American who boasts "I'm my own man" can expect to find his Japanese hosts anxiously counting the chopsticks after a business lunch. As the Japanese see it, individualists are anti-social. Team players are sound.

(from *The Economist*)

Decide whether these statements are true (✓) or false (✗), according to the article.

1 American managers learn about the cultural assumptions of the Japanese. ☐
2 In the eyes of Americans people who hesitate have something to hide. ☐
3 The Japanese are impressed by careful replies. ☐
4 Periods of silence bother the Japanese. ☐
5 Americans are embarrassed by conversations that stop. ☐
6 The Japanese are in favour of working in teams. ☐

Highlight any useful vocabulary you'd like to remember in the passage.

Ⓐ Welcome to Meridian International!

➡ Use the Workbook recording for this exercise.

◎◎ You're going to play the role of CHRIS STEINER. Imagine that you've just joined Meridian International and you'll be introduced to various people in the firm. Reply to each person when you hear the « *beep* » sound.

Look at this example and listen to the recording. Your role is printed **in bold type**:

Ted: Well, Jean, I'd like you to meet Chris Steiner. Chris, this is Jean Leroi, he's our export manager.

Mr Leroi: How do you do.

« *beep* »

YOU: **How do you do, Mr Leroi.**

Mr Leroi: Nice to meet you, Chris. How are you?

« *beep* »

YOU: **I'm fine, thanks. It's nice to meet you too.**

➡ You may need to PAUSE THE RECORDING to give yourself enough time to think before you speak.

Ⓑ What would you say?

What would you say in these situations? Write down the exact words you'd use. The first is done for you as an example.

1 The customer services manager, Mrs Hanson, doesn't know Linda Morris, the new export clerk.

   ...Mrs Hanson, I'd like you to meet Linda Morris. She's our new export clerk....

2 Your boss says to you, 'This is Tony Watson. He's visiting us from Canada.'

   ....

3 Tony Watson says, 'Hi. I think you know one of my colleagues: Ann Scott.'

   ....

4 You've been introduced to someone by name, but later in the conversation you can't remember the person's name.

   ....

5 You enter an office full of strangers one morning. Someone asks if they can help you.

   ....

6 A visitor arrives after travelling a long distance to see you.

   ....

7 Your visitor looks thirsty.

   ....

8 It's time for you to leave. You look at your watch and realize that it's later than you thought.

   ....

Questions keep a conversation going. Questions help you to find out more information from someone. Questions show someone that you're interested in what they have to say, and enjoy talking to them.

These exercises focus on forming questions correctly, and avoiding mistakes. Check your answers in the Answer Key after you've done each exercise.

A   Write down the QUESTIONS that led to each of these answers. The first is done for you as an example.

1   ...Are you Mrs Meier? ....   That's right. Pleased to meet you.
2   ....?   Yes, thanks, I had a very good flight.
3   ....?   I'd like to see Mr Perez, if he's in the office.
4   ....?   On my last visit I spoke to Ms Wong.
5   ....?   It was Mr Grün who recommended the hotel to me.
6   ....?   No, my husband is travelling with me. I'm meeting him later.
7   ....?   We'll probably be staying till Friday morning.
8   ....?   No, this is his first visit – he's never been here before.

➡   Check your answers before you do the next exercise.

B   Imagine that you're talking to someone who talks rather unclearly, and that you can't catch some of the information he or she gives you.
Write down the questions you'd ask this person to find out the missing (~~~~) information.

1   'I work for ~~~~.'   Who   *do you work for?*
2   'I live in ~~~~.'   Where   *do you live?*
3   'I've been working here for ~~~~ years.'   How   ?
4   'We keep our sales files in the ~~~~ room.'   Which   ?
5   'We never phone in the morning because ~~~~.'   Why   ?
6   'I started working for the firm in 19~~~~.'   When   ?
7   'I'd like a ~~~~ room for two nights, please.'   What kind of   ?
8   'I heard about this product from Mr ~~~~.'   Who   ?
9   'The complete package costs only $ ~~~~.'   How much   ?
10   'They printed ~~~~ thousand copies of the report.'   How many   ?
11   'They asked me to ~~~~ as soon as possible.'   What   ?
12   'Mrs ~~~~ told me I should get in touch with you.'   Who   ?

C   In these sentences the 'question tags' are missing, aren't they? Complete each sentence with a suitable question tag. The first two are done for you as examples.

1   They don't normally pay their account late, ...*do they?*...
2   The phone number is 518361, ...*isn't it?*...
3   They'll let us know before the end of the month, ...?
4   We can send the catalogues by surface mail, ...?
5   They can't provide us with the information we need, ...?
6   She isn't in the office today, ...?
7   This machine doesn't operate automatically, ...?
8   You know a great deal about economics, ...?
9   You've studied this subject for some time, ...?
10   We shouldn't interrupt the meeting, ...?
11   We must confirm this by sending them a fax, ...?
12   He hasn't heard that the firm has been taken over, ...?

Read this article and then answer the questions below.

Management in America

Do it my way

NEW YORK

Cultural differences between Japanese and American managers have presented the biggest obstacles to Japanese companies investing in America.

A seminar for Japanese executives working in America was attended by 25 men, nearly all of them in identical dark suits. Despite the room's stifling heating system, they resolutely refused to remove their jackets. Their coffee break lasted exactly the scheduled ten minutes. They did not' ask any questions until after they had got to know one another a bit better at lunch. They were usually deferential and always polite.

A similar seminar for 25 Americans working for Japanese subsidiaries in America included eight women. Several of the men removed their jackets on entering the room. A ten-minute coffee break stretched beyond 20 minutes. Participants asked questions and several aggressively contradicted what the speakers had to say.

According to Mr Thomas Lifson of Harvard and Mr Yoshihiro Tsurumi of New York's Baruch College – the two main speakers at both seminars – misunderstandings between Japanese and American managers are possible at nearly every encounter. They can begin at the first recruiting interview. A big American company typically hires people to fill particular slots. Its bosses know that Americans are mobile people, who have a limited commitment to any particular employer or part of the country. As a result, jobs are clearly defined and so are the skills needed to fill them. American firms hire and fire almost at will.

The assumptions (and the expectations) of the Japanese managers of Japanese subsidiaries in America could hardly be more different. They hire people more for the skills they will acquire after joining the company than for their existing skills.

American managers rely heavily on number-packed memoranda and the like. The Japanese colleagues prefer informal consultations which lead eventually to a consensus. According to Mr Tsurumi, they find comical the sight of American managers in adjacent offices exchanging memos.

Confronted with a dispute between middle managers, most Japanese superiors refuse to become involved, expecting the managers themselves to resolve the issue. The Americans conclude, wrongly, that their Japanese bosses are indecisive or incompetent. Japanese managers do not share the American belief that conflict is inevitable, and sometimes healthy. They want to believe that employees form one big happy family.

(from *The Economist*)

Decide whether these statements are true (✓) or false (✗), according to the article.

1 This article is about American companies in Japan.   ☐
2 At one seminar the Japanese removed their jackets when they got hot.   ☐
3 The Japanese did not ask questions until after lunch.   ☐
4 At another seminar, some of the Americans were not polite to the speakers.   ☐
5 Americans and Japanese are likely to misunderstand each other in any situation.   ☐
6 American employees are very loyal to their companies.   ☐
7 Japanese companies are likely to recruit less experienced employees.   ☐
8 The Japanese rely less on meetings than the Americans.   ☐
9 Japanese managers send more memos than their American counterparts.   ☐
10 Japanese managers solve problems without involving their boss.   ☐

abc Highlight any useful vocabulary you'd like to remember in the passage.

2 Letters, faxes and memos

2.1 A business letter   *Background information*

There are nine important parts in a typical 'standard' business letter – the example that follows shows these parts. Many firms use their own 'house style' which their staff are expected to follow, and which may not be quite the same as this example.

1 Sender's address (printed at the top or in the top right-hand corner)

Our company's name
This building
95 New Edition Road
Cambridge CB2 2RU
United Kingdom

3 Receiver's name, title and address

```
A. Reader
General Manager
International Business English plc
Page 000
Background information BA2 1LJ                    7 May 1999
```

2 Date (here or below the receiver's address)

4 Salutation

Dear Mr or Ms Reader,

5 Heading

Different ways of communicating in writing

6 Body of letter

In a LETTER, the emphasis is on a high quality appearance. Letters have to be typed or word-processed accurately on the company's headed paper with a smart, clear layout. International mail tends to be slow and in some countries the post is unreliable. Important documents or valuable items can be sent by registered mail – or they can be sent by courier.

A FAX is a facsimile copy of a document which is transmitted by normal telephone lines to another fax machine. Some faxes are exactly like letters, some are printed on special fax forms rather like memos, others are simply handwritten messages. The sender of a fax can't be certain if the message has been received perfectly – sometimes lines get missed or are illegible. A fax is not usually a legally binding document.

EMAIL (electronic mail) is a way of sending messages between computers. The message appears on a screen and can be printed out if necessary. To make email more 'personal' some people use punctuation to add happy {:-) or unhappy {:-(faces to their messages!

In a TELEX readers often overlook some errors of spelling and grammar. Abbreviations such as TKS (Thanks) and RGDS (Regards) are common in telexes. The sender knows when each telex has been transmitted and received. A telex can be a legally binding document.

Internal mail within a company or between branches of the same firm is usually in the form of MEMOS: these may be brief handwritten notes or longer, word-processed letters. Most firms use special memo pads for internal messages. A memo to a senior English-speaking member of staff may need as much care as a letter to a client. The style that is used depends on the practice within the company and on the relationship between the people involved.

Yours sincerely,

Leo Jones *Richard Alexander*

Leo Jones and Richard Alexander
Authors

* If there is a line space between each paragraph, the new paragraph needn't be indented.

7 Complimentary close

8 Signature

9 Name and title of sender

Vocabulary

Write the missing words in these sentences in the spaces in the puzzle. The first one is done for you as an example.

1 A .... layout is important in a letter.
2 I .... a cheque for £19.99.
3 An urgent document may be sent by .... instead of by mail.
4 *Your ref.* is short for Your ....
5 Remember to put the .... on a letter to the USA.
6 Remember to put the .... on a letter to the UK.
7 If you sign a letter on someone else's behalf, add the letters .... before the other person's name.
8 We .... receipt of your letter.
9 That flashing light means the .... is out of paper.
10 Letters used to be typed, but now they are ....
11 Paper, envelopes, paper clips, etc. are all items of ....
12 Memo is short for ....
13 If you make notes in .... you can erase them easily.
14 Valuable items can be sent by .... mail.
15 This unit is all about ....

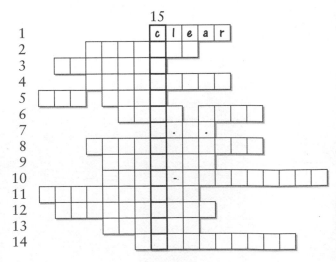

Unit 2   Letters, faxes and memos

A Study these rules and the examples.

> If we want to connect two or more ideas in a paragraph, we can do it in four different ways:
>
> **1** By using a **conjunction**:
>
> TIME: **and   before   after   while**
>
> REASON, CAUSE or RESULT: **and   because   so that   so ... that   such a ... that**
>
> CONTRAST: **but   although**
>
> I called her back *so that* I could confirm one or two details.
> The consignment was delivered *while* we were very busy.
> The goods were repacked *so* quickly *that* we had no time to inspect them.
>
> **2** By using a linking **adverbial phrase** (often starting a new sentence):
>
> TIME: **Before that   After that   And then   During this time**
>
> REASON, CAUSE or RESULT: **Because of this   That is why   As a result   Consequently**
>
> CONTRAST: **Nevertheless   However**
>
> I wanted to confirm one or two details. *That is why* I called her back.
> The consignment was delivered on Friday. *During this time* we were very busy.
> The goods were repacked at once. *Consequently* there was no time to inspect them.
>
> **3** By using a **preposition**:
>
> TIME: **before   after   during**
>
> REASON, CAUSE or RESULT: **because of   due to**
>
> CONTRAST: **in spite of**
>
> I called her back *because of* the need to confirm one or two details.
> The consignment was delivered *during* a very busy time.
> *Due to* our prompt repacking procedure, the goods were not inspected.
>
> **4** To show **PURPOSE**, an **infinitive clause** can also be used:
>
> The procedure has been computerized *in order to / so as to* save time and money.

➡ Compare your answers with the ones in the Answer Key after finishing each exercise.

B Join the two halves of these sentences so that they make good sense. The first is done for you as an example.

1 I never sign a letter   **although** a phone call is quicker.
2 I often choose to write   **after** I have checked our stock position.
3 I usually telephone   **before** I have read it through.
4 Please check my in-tray   **in order** to save time.
5 I shall be able to confirm this **because** we do not have sufficient stocks.
6 I shall be able to confirm this **until** we have checked our stock position.
7 We cannot confirm the order   **while** I am away at the conference.
8 Please reply at once   **so that** we can order the supplies we need.
9 Please reply as soon as possible **when** I have consulted our works manager.

C Rewrite these sentences beginning with the words shown. Again, the first is done for you as an example.

1 The reason why he applied for a job abroad was to earn more money.

So that he ...*could earn more money, he applied for a job abroad.*....

2 A single person couldn't lift the package because it was very heavy.

The package was so ....

3 The order arrived late but we were able to supply the goods on time.

Although ....

4 There was fog at the airport, but our plane landed safely.

In spite of ....

5 As there was a mistake in the hotel booking, I had to find another hotel.

Because of ....

6 The reason why I sent them a fax was to give them the information at once.

In order to ....

7 Because there has been an error in the shipping department, their order will have to be checked again.

Due to ....

8 During the time we've been talking, my assistant has handed me the file.

While ....

D Here are some paragraphs with very short sentences. Join the sentences together to make one or two longer sentences, using *and* and other conjunctions or adverbial phrases. The first is done for you as an example.

1 There was a technical problem. The assembly line stopped. The workers were sent home early.

> The workers were sent home early when the assembly line stopped due to a technical problem.

2 Your letter to us was posted yesterday. Our letter to you was posted yesterday. The letters crossed in the post.

3 Our company has a long tradition. Our letters look old-fashioned. We are trying to modernize the company's image. All our correspondence should be word-processed.

4 Short sentences are easy to write. Short sentences are easy to understand. Long words can be confusing. A simple style of writing letters is recommended.

5 A letter should have a personal touch. People like to be treated as individuals. It is unwise to use a style that is too informal with people you don't know very well.

E A long, complicated sentence may be confusing for a reader. Often short sentences are clearer. Rewrite each long sentence as 2 or 3 shorter sentences, beginning as suggested:

As requested, I enclose our new catalogue and feel sure that you will find within many items to interest you, particularly our new range of colours that will brighten up your office and keep your staff feeling happy.

> I am sending ...

Working in an export department requires a great deal of specialist knowledge, including a mastery of the complex documentation, an awareness of the various methods of payment that are available and the ability to correspond with customers in a distant country.

> If you work in ...

One of the most difficult aspects of corresponding with people you have not met face-to-face is establishing a personal relationship with them in order to show them that you are not just a letter-writing machine but a real person.

> Writing to people ...

2.4 Can you tell me how to spell that? *Speaking* ◎◎

A Look at the pairs of words below: one word in each pair is wrongly spelt, the other correctly spelt.
Decide which spellings are correct and cross out the incorrect ones.

B ◎◎ Play the recording and PAUSE it after each number. Then spell the correct word out loud, like this:

Recorded voice: One.
YOU – PAUSE *the recording, then speak:* 'A - C - K - N - O - W - L - E - D - G - E' – *Then release PAUSE.*
Recorded voice giving model answer: Acknowledge: A - C - K - N - O - W - L - E - D - G - E.

1 ~~acknowlege~~ acknowledge
2 accommodation acommodation
3 aquire acquire
4 across accross
5 adress address
6 altogether alltogether
7 approximatively approximately
8 independent independant

9 itinerery itinerary
10 permanent permanant
11 pronounciation pronunciation
12 received recieved
13 reccomend recommend
14 recipient recipiant
15 seperate separate

A This extract has 13 spelling mistakes. Find the mistakes and correct them.

```
Dear Madame,

Thank you very much for your letter and the inclosed
literature, wich we recieved on Thursday 7 July.
The infomation it contained was quiet interesting
and we would like futher details on several produkts
in the cataloge:

No. 44/77        Is this availaible in white?
No. 78/612       What is the diskount price of this
                 for orders of over 500 peices?
No. 34/009       Is this compatable with your 55/88
                 device?
```

B This extract has several punctuation mistakes. Find the mistakes and correct them.

```
I am afraid, that we have not been able to contact
you by telephone  My secretary called throughout the
day yesterday at half hourly-interval's but was told
that you were not available"; please contact me
personally as soon as possible. Because we need to
check a number of detail's in your order?

You can reach me by telephone at any time this
afternoon or tomorrow morning. Our office hours' are
8.30 to 5 you can leave a message for me, to call
you back if necessary.
```

➡ There are two mistakes in the title too. Did you spot them?

2.6 Abbreviations *Vocabulary*

Replace the abbreviations with complete words.

1 Just as **Rd** is short for ...Road..., **St** and **Sq** are short for .... and ....
2 **12/7/99** means .... 1999 in Britain but it means .... 1999 in America.
3 **#24** in the USA and **No. 24** in Britain both mean .... 24.
4 On an envelope **c/o** means .... and **Attn** means that the letter is for the .... of a particular person.

5 In a report or textbook **e.g.** or **eg** means ...., **i.e.** or **ie** means
.... and **etc.** or **etc** stands for ....

6 A British firm's name may be followed by the abbreviation **plc** or **PLC** (short for
.......................), **Ltd** (.......................) or **& Co.** (.......................).

7 An American firm's name may be followed by **Corp.** (.......................) or **Inc.**
(.......................).

8 If you buy something by mail order the price may not include **p & p**
(.......................) and **VAT** (.......................).

9 At the end of a business letter you may see the abbreviations **c.c.** (.......................),
enc. or **encl.** (.......................). But only an informal letter would have a **P.S.**
(.......................) at the end.

10 What do these abbreviations stand for?
@ ¥3,000 ea. ....
© Cambridge University Press 1996 ....
Apple® Macintosh™ ....
WYSIWYG ....

2.7 Make a good impression   *Writing*

We think you'll agree that this letter doesn't make a very good impression on the reader.

❶ Decide what parts can be improved to give a better impression.

❷ Rewrite the letter in your own words.

❸ Compare your version with the letter in the Answer Key.

> Dear Mr Brown,
>
> What an unexpected pleasure to hear from you
> after all this time! We thought you must have
> forgotten us since you placed your previous
> order with us two years ago.
>
> May I take this opportunity of enclosing for
> your attention our new catalogue and price
> lists. One of the things you'll probably notice
> is that all the prices have gone up by 15%
> since your last order but still, never mind,
> everyone else's have gone up too — even yours I
> expect! Nevertheless, for your current order,
> we shall be delighted to supply you at the old
> price, so you're quite lucky.
>
> Oh, and another thing, I nearly forgot: you can
> contact us by fax if you feel like it. The
> number is 998321, all right?
>
> So, there we are, nice to be writing to you
> again.
>
> Yours faithfully,
>
> A. Burke
> Sales Director

3 On the phone

3.1 Business calls   *Background information*

If you don't have much experience of making phone calls in English, making a business call can be a worrying experience. If you have to call someone you already know, you may actually enjoy making the call – but remember that long-distance calls are expensive.

Or you may have to make a first-time business call to a prospective client: not easy in English! Making a phone call to a stranger can be quite stressful, especially if they speak English better than you.

Most business people, unless they feel *very* confident, prepare for an important phone call in a foreign language by making notes in advance. And during the call they make notes while they're talking to help them to remember what was said.

Although it's quick and convenient to phone someone to give them information or to ask questions, the disadvantage is that there is nothing in writing to help you to remember what was said. It's essential to make notes and often when an agreement is reached on the phone, one of the speakers will send a fax to confirm the main points that were made.

As it's so easy to be misunderstood when talking on the phone it's a good idea to repeat any important information (especially numbers and names) back to the other person to make sure you've got it right. Always make sure you know the name of the person you're talking to. If necessary, ask them to spell it out to you, so that you can make sure you've got it right – and try to use their name during the call. And make sure they know *your* name too.

It's important to sound interested, helpful and alert when answering the phone. You may have to make or receive calls to or from regular customers and prospective customers, so a good telephone manner not only makes an impression in business, but it also helps to make money.

3.2 Telephone techniques   *Listening* ◎◎

◎◎ You'll hear part of a talk in which a training officer is giving advice to some trainees on telephone techniques. Listen to the recording and fill the gaps in this summary:

1 Identify yourself by giving your ___name___ and your _____ in the company.
2 Make sure you're talking to the _____ _____

3 Say right away what you're calling about. Be ▨▨▨▨▨, and don't waste time.
4 If it's a ▨▨▨▨ ▨▨▨▨▨, say that you'll ▨▨▨▨ ▨▨▨▨ at once. Then start the call again.
5 Speak slowly and clearly, but in a friendly voice. ▨▨▨▨ while you're speaking.
6 Don't use ▨▨▨▨ terms or ▨▨▨▨, because the other person may not understand these as well as you do.
7 Give important information, like figures, ▨▨▨▨, ▨▨▨▨, dates and so on, slowly and carefully.
8 Don't ▨▨▨▨ the other person even if you think you know what he or she is going to say.
9 Don't phone during the other person's ▨▨▨▨ ▨▨▨▨ – find out what time it is in the other country before you call.
10 ▨▨▨▨ ▨▨▨▨ all the important information you're given by the other person.

Vocabulary

Fill the gaps with suitable words from the list.

area code   busy (US) / *engaged* (GB)   *collect call* (US) / *transferred charge call* (GB)
dialing (US) / *dialling* (GB)   *off the hook*
person-to-person call (US) / *personal call* (GB)   *ringing*

1 To make a call: first listen for the .... tone and dial the number. With any luck, you'll hear a tone telling you that the number is .... If the other phone is being used you'll hear the .... tone.
2 To make an international call: first dial the international code, then the country code, then the .... and finally the number you require.
3 If you want the other person to pay for the call you can make a ....
4 If you want to talk to a particular person you can make a ....
5 If you don't want to be interrupted, you can leave the phone ....

Speaking ◎◎

These exercises are all recorded on the Workbook recording.

Before you play the recording, look at the examples – what you say is printed **in bold type**. Then do the recorded exercise.
You should pause the recording if you need to think before you speak.

Ⓐ ◎◎ **What would you like me to get you?**

Colleague: I'm just going to the coffee machine. Would you like some coffee ... or a cold drink?
« *beep* »
YOU: **Oh, yes, please. Could you get me some coffee, please?**
Colleague: How would you like it: black or white?
« *beep* »
YOU: **I'd like black, please.**
Colleague: Sure, OK.

➡ Always ask for the FIRST alternative your colleague offers.

B 🔊 Can you help me?

You'll hear some people making requests, offering to help you or asking for your permission. Agree or refuse, according to the instructions given in the recording.

Colleague: Um, I wonder if you could lend me an umbrella? I need to go out for a little while.
« beep »
YOU: **Why certainly, I'd be glad to. Mine's over there.**
Colleague: Would you mind telling me how to put it up?
« beep »
YOU: **Sure, you just press this button here.**
Colleague: I'm expecting a call from Tokyo at 1.30. I'd like you to take a message for me, please.
« poop »
YOU: **I'm sorry, but I'll be having lunch at 1.30.**

C 🔊 Mr Brown, is it all right if I ...?

Imagine that your boss's name is Mr Brown, and your own name is Chris. You need to ask Mr Brown's permission to do various things.

Colleague: If you want to leave the office at 4.30 this afternoon, you should ask Mr Brown.
Mr Brown: Yes, Chris?
« beep »
YOU: **Excuse me, Mr Brown, is it all right if I leave the office at 4.30 this afternoon?**
Mr Brown: 4.30? Oh, yes, that should be OK.
« beep »
YOU: **Oh, thanks very much, Mr Brown.**

3.5 Speaking and writing   *Functions*

Imagine that you're writing a letter to a client. Write down the words you would write in place of these sentences which were spoken on the phone.

1 'Oh, do you think you could call me about this next week?'
   Could ...*you please telephone me about this next week?*..

2 'Do you think you could confirm this by fax?'
   Would ....

3 'Sorry, but we can't give you a special discount.'
   I regret to say that ....

4 'If you like, we can send you a sample of this product.'
   Please let us know if ....

5 'Will it be OK to ship the order in two separate consignments?'
   With your permission, we propose ....

6 'Thanks a lot for all your help. It was very kind of you.'
   Thank you ....

7 'There may be some questions about our literature – if so, can I help at all?'
   If you ....

8 'Terribly sorry, but you can't amend an order over the phone.'
   Unfortunately, ...

Add the missing words to the puzzle.

1 Hello. This is Louise Bonnard ..... Can I help you?
2 Could you .... the line for a moment, please?
3 Hello, switchboard? Can I have an ...., please?
4 What is Miss Fisher's .... number?
5 Can I leave a .... for Sarah Grey, please?
6 To make a call from a public telephone, lift the ....
   and insert a coin.
7 I'm sorry, I can't hear you very well, this is a ....
8 Could you give me a .... tomorrow morning?
9 The number for .... enquiries in the UK is 192.
10 She's in a meeting, I'm afraid. Can I be of any ....?
11 Some public phones take coins, others take ....

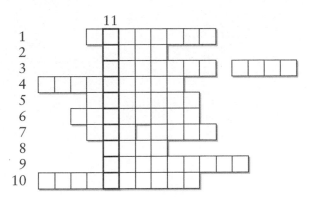

3.7 Three messages   *Listening & note-taking* ◎◎

◎◎ You'll hear three messages which you are taking on behalf of your colleague, Mr Collins. Listen to the recording and fill the gaps in these notes.

➡ After each message compare your notes with the answers in the Key – and then listen to the recording again to check again on any mistakes you made.

1

SUSAN GRANT of Richmond Studios called about order
for 1 x MQ 20, sent 3 weeks ago – on _____ of
this month.
Sent you cheque for £ _____ to get it at special
offer price but no _____ of order.
Please confirm receipt of order and _____
Any problems, phone Susan Grant on 0303 _____
When can she expect _____?
Address: _____ High Street, Woodbridge,
_____, IP12 4SJ

2

PETER _____ of Eastern Enterprises in _____
called:
Can't _____ on _____ afternoon
because of problem with hotel – no room because of
_____
All other hotels in town full because of _____
Will come on Monday morning (_____) if OK with you.
Please tell him if this change of date is _____
Please call him if you have ideas for _____
_____ on 617

3

_____ called:
Staying 2 extra days in _____ and trying to
get flight back on _____. Direct flight is full – they've put him
on _____
May not be back till _____
If not back, please take over at meeting on Tuesday with
_____
All info in file on his desk with _____'s name on.
Please collect O.F. from _____ Hotel first thing
in the morning.
Any problem: leave a message at his hotel
(_____) or send fax (_____)

3.8 Call me back   *Vocabulary*

A Decide which of these phrases fit best in the following sentences.

be over   call back   cut off   get through   give up   hang up   hold on   look up
pick up   put through

1 The phone's ringing. Why don't you .... the receiver?
2 I'm afraid she isn't available at the moment. Can you .... later?
3 Can you .... their number in the directory, please?
4 I'm afraid she's with a client, shall I .... you .... to her secretary?
5 Hello? Are you still there? I think we were .... for a moment.
6 Mr Green never seems to be in his office. I've been trying to .... to him all morning.
7 Could you .... for a moment? I'll just find out for you.
8 If the telephonist says *'Thank you so much for calling'* and plays me that awful electronic music again, I'll ....
9 If you get a wrong number, it's polite to say *'I'm sorry, I've dialled the wrong number'* before you ....
10 If an American telephonist asks *'Are you through?'*, she wants to know if your call ....

B Now fill the gaps in **A** with these words and phrases:

be finished   connect with   disconnect   find   lift   reach   replace the receiver
return the call   stop trying   wait

3.9 Present tenses   *Grammar review*

A Study this summary before you do the exercises that follow.

---

1 The **present simple** refers to 'permanent states or situations' and to 'regular happenings or habits':

> We always *file* the documents here and *send* copies to head office.
> He *lives* in London but *spends* every other week in New York.
> *Does* your company *deal* with the Far East?

Here are some typical adverbs you can use with the present simple:

> *always   generally   occasionally   frequently   sometimes   often   usually*
> *normally   on a regular basis   regularly   twice a year   once a week*
> *every year   every two weeks   every other month   once in a while*
> *from time to time   never   rarely   hardly ever   seldom*

2 The **present progressive** refers to 'temporary, developing or changing situations':

> While *she's looking* for accommodation, *she's staying* with us.
> The market outlook for North America *is getting* better.
> *Is* anyone *taking* Mr Rossi's calls while *he's working* at home?

Some typical adverbs:

> *at the moment   now   just now   right now   today   presently (US & Scots)*
> *at present   this morning   for the moment*

3 Some verbs (known as 'stative verbs') are NOT normally used with the present progressive:

> I *realize* that their product *costs* less than ours, but ...

> I *believe* he still *owes* us quite a lot of money.
> *Do you remember* how much each parcel *weighs*?
> Each package that we are sending *contains* 12 items.
> Our rate of discount *depends* on the quantity you order.
>
> Typical verbs:
>
> *appear believe belong consist of contain cost depend on deserve*
> *fit lack like look like matter measure owe own prefer realize*
> *remember understand weigh*

B Fill the gaps in the sentences, using the verbs in this list:

assist attend call back deserve get through
look up make pick up print out put through

1 Normally she ...**calls back**... straight away.
2 His secretary always .... the phone first.
3 This year we .... to get a pay rise.
4 This week he .... the Personnel Director with the interviews.
5 She .... the number in the phone book at the moment.
6 Today I .... a training session on quality control.
7 Once a week the computer .... the sales figures.
8 We hardly ever .... to Bombay so easily.
9 Please hold on. I .... to the Sales Department.
10 I .... some notes now and I'll make the call in a few minutes.

C Imagine that you're being given information over the phone, but that it's a bad line.
Write down the QUESTIONS you'd ask to find out the missing information.

1 The consignment consists of ~~~~ pieces.
   Sorry, **how many pieces does the consignment consist of?**
2 We usually keep in touch with him by ~~~~.
   I'm sorry, how .... ?
3 The ~~~~ shipment is being unpacked now.
   Sorry, which .... ?
4 This specification looks exactly like ~~~~.
   Pardon? What .... ?
5 She's working in ~~~~ at present.
   Excuse me, where .... ?

D Imagine that you're being given some information over the phone that is incorrect.
Write down what you'd say to the other person to let them know they're wrong.

1 The parcel weighs 500 kilos, I think.
   Well, no, actually ...**it doesn't weigh 500 kilos.**...
2 You're making up the order this week, I gather.
   Well, no, in fact ....
3 I suppose the computer prints out the figures every day.
   Well, no, actually ....
4 You're working now as Mrs Green's assistant, aren't you?
   Well, no, in actual fact ....
5 They always deliver the goods promptly, I believe.
   Well, no, actually ....

4 Summaries, notes, reports

4.1 Writing reports   *Background information*

In business, planning and writing reports, making summaries and taking notes are important skills which may be expected of everyone. We tend only to write reports when we are asked to, usually by our boss or superior. Many people are afraid of writing reports. There is no good reason for this. It's often simply a question of stopping and thinking about what it is you have to do and then doing it. And it is a question of practice.

It is important to remember that there are several types of report. They can be long, short, formal or informal and they can be spoken or written as:

– conversations
– letters
– memos
– special forms
– separate documents of several pages

Reports can serve various purposes. There are reports which inform, reports which provide background information to help someone make up their mind about something and there are reports which in themselves make recommendations or indicate a course of action.

There are many things you should do before you even think about 'writing' or drafting the report. You should first prepare or assemble your material and then plan

how you are going to write the report. The preparation and writing of a report falls into four stages:

1 Assembling the material
2 Planning the report
3 Drafting the report
4 Editing the report

Any report – on the page – has three main 'parts' which must include four (sometimes five or even six) essential elements:

Parts	*Elements*
Introduction	{ Terms of reference or objective Procedure
Body of the report	Findings
Final section	{ Conclusions (Recommendations if asked for) (Appendices)

This structure should be evident in every report. In some cases you may need to have elements such as appendices, etc. at the end. For students of Business English the three main parts can have these headings:

Introduction
Facts
Conclusions

Read the following text. Decide where to add punctuation and to start new paragraphs. You'll also need to add some Capital Letters.

```
to departmental manager from human resources manager date 15 september
subject overseas trainee placement scheme as requested i enclose a copy of
the scheduled programme for the trainee initiation week it will be held
from 23 october to 27 october following your secretarys telephone call i have
set aside a session for you to speak to the participants i have scheduled
this for monday 23 october starting at 3 00 pm i am now completing the final
arrangements for the week accordingly i would be grateful if you could
confirm that the proposed time on monday will be convenient for you in
addition i would also appreciate receiving any comments you may have on the
programme by friday of this week if possible
```

4.3 Summarizing   *Listening & speaking*. ◎◎

Ⓐ ◎◎ Listen to the recording. In Conversation 1 a woman talks about an experience she had, and in Conversation 2 you will hear three people talking.

Conversation 1

1 How do you think the person feels in this recording? Why do you think this is the case?
2 Pause the recording when you hear the « *beep* » tone.
3 Summarize out loud briefly what happened.
4 Restart the recording and see if the spoken summary is close to your own or not.
5 What other points would you add?

Conversation 2

1 In this recording, what sort of mood would you say the people are in? What is the reason for this?
2 Pause the recording when you hear the « *beep* » tone.
3 Summarize out loud briefly what happened.
4 Restart the recording and see if the spoken summary is close to your own or not.

Ⓑ ◎◎ Conversations 3 and 4

Now listen to two more conversations. When you hear the « *beep* » tone, stop the recording and write a short summary of each conversation using your own words.

When you look at the Answer Key, remember there is no 'best version' of a summary.

Conversation 3	Conversation 4

4.4 Getting it down on paper *Vocabulary*

Add the missing words to the puzzle.

1 Put the name of the .... at the top of the memo.
2 When it is finished send or .... the report to the person who asks for it.
3 When you take a message try to keep it ....
4 A top manager is an .... of the company.
5 Only .... the main points of a message.
6 First .... or put in a particular order the things you want to say, before you start.
7 Make a first .... of anything you write and then correct it.
8 .... should only contain one main idea.
9 The .... is a punctuation mark with two dots.
10 Remember to .... your spelling before you type the report.
11 The punctuation mark that looks like a 'flying comma' is called the ....
12 When you report facts make sure you are ....
13 A letter used inside a firm is called a ....
14 .... is another word for full stop.
15 A .... is something that gets sent around to many people.

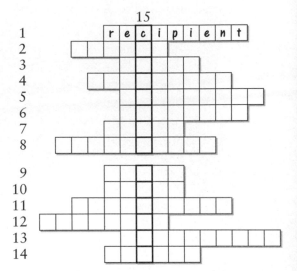

4.5 Dealing with a report *Reading*

A The paragraphs of Anita Fuchsberger's report got mixed up on the word processor and they were not numbered. Number the correct order you think they should be in. One is done for you as an example.

MEMO

From: Anita Fuchsberger
To: Felicitas Zapp

Quarterly Report on Office Furniture

3 The first point to stress is that following the acquisition of the Relaxo Group and J. S. Moretti S.p.A. last year, Relaxo International, the renamed division, experienced a year of consolidation and profit growth this year.

Relaxo Systems Furniture in the UK continued its profitable growth pattern. In marketing terms, the major events include extensions to the System M100 screen based furniture range which is proving such a popular product with major British companies. New storage products were also introduced in October. Alhambra, a Spanish desking range, was launched in the UK for the front office furniture market. It was well received and projected sales for next year are encouraging.

Muebles Relax de España showed real profit improvement following the factory investments which have led to more cost-effective manufacture. The order book increased significantly during the year, despite the lack of any real improvement in the business climate in Spain. This was due to the introduction of new desking and storage products, aided by key changes to the sales management structure.

I must apologize for the late submission of my report, but the delay was partly connected with my visit to our Spanish subsidiary in San Sebastian. I had to step in at the last moment for the Sales Manager, who unfortunately suffered a car accident.

Overall, the past year has been a favourable one for the Relaxo Group in all three European regions. This has been the case despite the variable conditions from country to country. The prospects for the coming years look favourable on the whole, and only the situation in the USA may give some cause for concern.

At the same time marketing activity was strengthened by the opening of new showrooms for Relaxo at the new International Design Centre in New York City and for Moretti S.p.A. in the office and factory complex just outside Milan. We also had good production results to show in our three major European regions: the Iberian Peninsula, Northern Europe and the British Isles.

Here are the results of my analysis of the international performance of Relaxo International together with some predictions for the future development of the business furniture market.

The Relaxo companies in Europe traded exceptionally well during the year, and new products were introduced to extend the System 99 executive seating range. The market conditions in Germany and Holland were very favourable and Relaxo looks able to take further advantage of this with systems furniture to be launched in these countries in the next couple of years. The Swiss company continues to develop its own markets and last year significantly increased its activity in southern Europe. However, market conditions in the USA were not so favourable for Relaxo Incorporated, but the opening of the showroom in New York should indicate a return to growth in the USA in coming years.

B Read the report again and decide which of the statements are true or false:

1 Anita Fuchsberger wishes she had not had to take the place of the Sales Manager in San Sebastian.
2 Anita Fuchsberger reports on the development of the business furniture market in the past few years.
3 The newly restructured company had a good year.
4 Production facilities were improved in America and Italy.
5 There were more orders in Spain during the year.
6 The success of the Spanish subsidiary was connected to the change in the business climate.
7 European trade developments helped Relaxo companies to expand the number of new products they were able to sell.
8 Anita Fuchsberger is not sure whether it will be an advantage to introduce new products in the next few years.
9 Relaxo Incorporated are likely to do less well in the USA in the future than they have this year.
10 The most important market development for the UK-based company was the introduction of the Alhambra desking range.

Read this article and then fill each gap below with one word.

RULE NUMBER ONE: CLEAR THAT DESK

If your desk is piled high with letters, faxes, forms, memos, reports, print-outs and sticky-backed message slips, you might believe all this paperwork is a sign of how busy you are. But according to Declan Treacy, cluttered desks lead to lost information, distractions, missed opportunities, high stress and not a little procrastination. He founded and runs the Clear Your Desk Organisation and organises the annual International Clear Your Desk Day which this year is being held on April 24.

His arguments for uncluttered desks are strong. 'We pile between 300 and 500 pieces of paper on the desk at any one time, a load equivalent to a 40-hour backlog of work. With 45 minutes a day wasted on frustrating searches for lost paperwork on and around the desk, it is unfortunate that the cluttered desk is the accepted norm in most organisations,' he says. Treacy holds seminars to help companies organise their own Clear Your Desk days, when everyone from the senior managers to secretaries learn how to tackle paperwork more effectively.

Paper has become the foundation on which our organisations are built and at the beginning of the 1990s office workers around the world were using more than 15 million miles of paper every day. Over two billion business letters are posted daily worldwide. In the US, companies have over 300 billion pieces of paper on file.

While a large proportion of this paperwork is important, we have reached a situation where most organisations, both public and private, are suffocating under mountains of unwanted paper. The average British worker hoards 40 hours of unfinished paperwork at any one time; each piece of paper on the desk will distract us up to five times a day; 68 per cent of office workers admit to habitually handling paperwork several times before deciding what to do with it; worldwide, computer printers produce over two and a half million pieces of paper every minute; 60 million photocopies are made every hour; 30 billion faxes are sent every year; and we hoard an average 20,000 pieces of paper in the office.

So what is someone to do if they have what looks like the EU paper mountain on their desk? Dump it in the bin? Well, yes, says Treacy. Or rather, he suggests following four simple rules, and dumping the stuff is number four. Rule number three is file it. Number two suggests passing it to someone else; number one is the rule no one will like: act on it.

What you shouldn't do is add to the pile of paper that's already there, says Treacy: 'Eighty per cent of all paperwork is eventually discarded, but it causes an awful lot of trouble before that happens. Unfortunately, most executives believe the myth that an empty desk is the sign of an unproductive mind. How wrong can you be? Companies cannot afford to let people work from cluttered desks. Hours of valuable time are wasted in searching for vital pieces of paper, and in being distracted by the constant stream of faxes, memos and reports which land in our in-trays when we should be devoting time to more important work.'

And what is Treacy's desk like? Perfectly clear, of course.

Susan Pape

(from *InterCity Magazine*)

1 According to Declan Treacy, an untidy desk is .... a sign of a busy person at work. The best kind of desk is a .... one.
2 International Clear Your Desk Day is held every ....
3 Office workers waste .... minutes a day looking for documents.
4 In most businesses an .... desk is considered perfectly acceptable.
5 It would take the average British worker .... hours to clear his or her desk of paperwork.
6 2½ million pieces of paper are printed by computers every .... and 60 million photocopies are made every ....
7 Treacy's four rules for clearing your desk of papers are:
    1 .... on it.
    2 .... it on to someone else.
    3 .... it.
    4 .... it away.

A Study the examples and the explanation which follows.

1 Look at these questions and the pairs of answers. What is the difference in emphasis between each of the pairs of answers? Decide which answer goes with which question.

> 1 Have you done anything about a room?
> 2 What about a room for the night?
> 3 Do we need capital?
> 4 What about capital?
> 5 Have you sent the consignment?
> 6 What has happened to the consignment?

> a A room has been reserved for you at the Grand Hotel.
> b We have booked a room for you at the Grand Hotel.
>
> c The consignment was sent last week, so you should receive it soon.
> d We sent the consignment last week, so you should get it soon.
>
> e No capital is required if your company is well known.
> f You don't need any capital if your company is well known.

2 In the examples above we see that the difference in focus between each of the pairs of sentences is fairly straightforward. So what is the passive used for?

Using the passive

We use the passive in English if we don't want to draw attention to the person who is responsible for a particular action or process. Indeed, the passive is very useful when you want to emphasize the object to which the action or process is happening rather than the person carrying out the action. So we can say:

> The passive is used in English to focus on the action.

Here it is *the process or use of the passive* we are interested in and not *who* is carrying out the process or using the passive (i.e. speakers of English). Consider some further examples:

> *Company targets* are set every year.
> *The factory* was set up in 1985.

In these sentences, we're focusing on *the company targets* or *the factory* and we're probably more interested in *when* the actions happened than in *who* carried them out. We can of course leave in *who* is doing the action. We do this by adding *by*. For example:

> *Production targets* were met by the workforce.

The focus is on the *production targets*, but at the same time we mention who they were met by, without emphasizing it.

B Rewrite each sentence, starting with the words given, so that it means the same as the preceding sentence.

1 The corporation's sales and service organization covers the country.
The country ...is covered by the corporation's sales and service organization...

2 We enclose payment together with our order.
Payment ....

3 The customer should receive the delivery by Friday.
The delivery ....

4 They may have notified him before the invoice arrived.
He ....

5 FCS are only marketing their new dental equipment in Europe.
FCS's new dental equipment ....

6 They have enlarged the premises since my last visit.
The premises ....

7 According to a recent report the group is making similar investments in other parts of the world.
Similar investments ....

8 The temporary clerk finally found the notes under the filing cabinet.
The notes ....

9 We will produce the components at our São Paolo factory.
The components ....

10 We would reduce costs if we used less paper.
Costs ....

C Rewrite these passive sentences in the active form. Begin with the word(s) given.

1 The first fax machines were installed in 1988.
The firm   installed its first fax machines in 1988.

2 Further modifications will be made to this service to other customers.
The suppliers

3 The systems can easily be operated by ordinary office staff.
Ordinary office staff

4 The new software can be mastered easily in a couple of days.
You

5 Increased productivity has been achieved by using better trained staff.
Using better trained staff

6 The invoices are now sent out a week earlier.
The department

7 Better results can only be achieved if you work harder.
You

8 The new note-taking method will be introduced in our office.
We

9 You should be warned about the dangers of not co-operating with the personnel manager.
I

10 All relevant information about the meeting will be supplied in advance.
The organizers

5 Working together

5.1 Different kinds of companies   *Background information*

There may be occasions when you have to talk about the company (*US English:* corporation) you work for. This may be when you're actually showing someone around the place of work or premises. Or you may need to explain to someone how your company or your department is organized, who is responsible for different aspects of the business and how the company is run.

Companies and corporations

Companies are a very important part of a country's economy. Businesses produce goods and services, and they come in every shape and size. Although the vast majority of the world's companies are small, in many countries the economy is dominated by large firms. Large businesses differ from small ones in a wide variety of ways. In many countries there are nationalized companies belonging to the state, as well as private companies. A private company might be a small firm with just one owner or a very large firm with thousands of shareholders 'owning' the firm.

In very large firms the shareholders have very little to do with the day-to-day running of the firm. This is left to the management. Large companies may be organized into several large departments, sometimes even divisions. The organizational structure of some companies is very hierarchical with a board of directors at the top and the various departmental heads reporting to them. Often the only time shareholders can influence the board is at the yearly shareholders' meeting.

Some firms may only produce one good or service. Others may produce many different products; in fact they may seem to be like a collection of 'businesses' inside one company. As a company gets bigger it may expand geographically. Many large firms are multinationals with manufacturing plants and trading locations in several different countries spread around the world.

Offices

The physical surroundings of most modern places of work, especially offices, are becoming more and more similar. Although there are some differences from country to country, one office looks much like another. Office furniture and equipment tends to be similar – desks, chairs, lamps, filing cabinets, computers, phones, photocopiers, etc.

The 'atmosphere' of the workplace can influence the effectiveness of a company's employees. Modern offices are more spacious and better lit, heated, ventilated and air-conditioned than in the past. But of course this is a feature that varies from firm to firm and may be dependent on the size of the company and its corporate 'philosophy'. In some companies, the employees work in large open-plan offices without walls between the departments. In others, the staff work more privately in individual offices.

Work relations with other people at the place of work include relationships with fellow employees, workers or colleagues. A great part of work or job satisfaction – some people say the major portion – comes from 'getting on' with others at work. Work relations will also include those between management and employees. These relations are not always straightforward, particularly as the management's assessment of how you're performing can be crucial to your future career.

Industrial relations

There will always be matters about which employees will want to talk to the management. In small businesses the boss will probably work alongside his or her workers. Anything which needs to be sorted out will be done face-to-face as soon as a problem arises. There will be no formal meetings or procedures. The larger the business, the less direct contact there will be between employees and management. Special meetings have to be held and procedures set up, to say when, where, how and in what circumstances the employees can talk to the management. Some companies have specially organized consultative committees for this purpose.

In many countries of the world today, particularly in large firms, employees join a trade union and ask the union to represent them to the management. Through the union all categories of employees can pass on the complaints they have and try to get things changed. The process through which unions negotiate with management on behalf of their members is called 'collective bargaining'. Instead of each employee trying to bargain alone with the company, the employees join together and collectively put forward their views. Occasionally a firm will refuse to recognize the right of a union to negotiate for its members and a dispute over union recognition will arise.

Where there is disagreement, bargaining or negotiating will take place. A compromise agreement may be reached. Where this is not possible, the sides can go to arbitration and bring in a third party from outside to say what they think should happen. However, sometimes one of the sides decides to take industrial action. The management can 'lock out' the employees and prevent them from coming to work. This used to be quite common, but is rarely used today.

The main courses of action open to a trade union are: a strike, a ban on working overtime, 'working to rule' (when employees work according to the company rule book), 'go-slows' (employees may spend more time doing the same job) and picketing (employees stand outside the entrance to the business location holding up signs to show that they are in conflict with the management).

Every country has its own tradition of industrial relations, so it is difficult to generalize. In some businesses, unions are not welcomed by the management. But in other countries the unions play an important role both in the everyday working relations in individual companies and also in the social and political life of the country.

5.2 Firms at work   *Vocabulary*

Add the missing words to the puzzle.

1 Several companies are .... in the development.
2 Ltd stands for .... company.
3 Mining and farming are part of the primary ....
4 Shops and supermarkets are part of the .... industry.

5 Our economy depends on private .... to combine capital and opportunities for investment.
6 The two firms want to .... to form a larger one.
7 We are moving because our business .... are too small.
8 The report shows our company had another .... year.
9 All the computer .... are linked to the main computer.
10 The .... joins the computer to the phone.
11 The .... department looks after the company's figures.
12 Another word for a a computer screen is ....
13 In America a large firm is called a ....

14 In American companies a director is called a ....

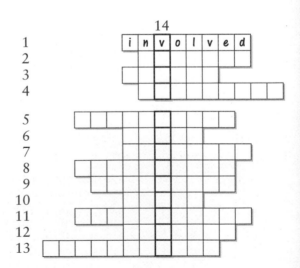

This is the first of six sections on word-building. The others are: 7.5, 9.4, 11.6, 13.3 and 15.4.

New words can be formed in English by adding prefixes to other words.

If you add them to other words they change the meaning, like this:

e.g.   organize   →   reorganize
         pronounce   →   mispronounce
         standard   →   sub-standard

Ⓐ Which of these meanings go with the prefixes below?

1 'again'/'back'   4 'many'   7 'wrongly'/'incorrectly'/'inefficiently'
2 'before'   5 'past'/'beyond'   8 'across'
3 'below'/'under'   6 'too much'

mis-   out-   over-   multi-   pre-   sub-   re-   trans-

Ⓑ Look through these sentences and fill the gap with a word built from the list on the right and a prefix from above.

1 The fall in the value of the dollar will mean a poor ...*outlook*...for the tourist trade this year.   **look**
2 Because the machine had .... its usefulness, the production manager proposed .... it.   **live**
   place
3 Our company can supply you with reply cards which are usually .... to suit standard situations.   **print**
4 The finance department badly .... the costings for the new factory buildings.   **calculate**
5 There's something wrong with this bill. I think they've .... me.   **charge**
6 We've received so many complaints about the product that we'll have to .... the next model.   **design**
7 Our major supplier is a large .... company, which always delivers on time.   **national**
8 Manufacture of the components was .... to a smaller company.   **contract**
9 If the rent is too big for the firm, they'll .... part of the site to another company.   **let**
10 Industrial buildings are sometimes .... in a factory and then assembled on site.   **fabricate**

◎◎ Listen to the recording:

❶ First read through the examples in speech balloons in **5.5 Ⓒ** in the Student's Book.
You're going to hear four conversations in which a number of men and women agree and disagree about different suggestions concerning working life.
Listen to each conversation twice.

❷ As you listen the first time, write down the *topic* of the conversation or the *suggestion* the people are talking about. Then listen a second time.

❸ Listen again and decide which of the people agree or disagree with the topic or proposal.
Put a ✓ for the people who AGREE or a ✗ for those who DISAGREE.

Conversation 1

TOPIC: ..Smoking should be.......
...forbidden in offices...........

1st woman	☑
1st man	☑
2nd woman	☒
2nd man	☐
3rd man	☐
3rd woman	☐

Conversation 3

TOPIC: ....
....

1st man	☐
1st woman	☐
2nd man	☐
2nd woman	☐
3rd man	☐
4th man	☐
3rd woman	☐

Conversation 2

TOPIC: ....
....

1st man	☐
1st woman	☐
2nd man	☐
2nd woman	☐
3rd man	☐
4th man	☐
3rd woman	☐

Conversation 4

TOPIC: ....
....

1st man	☐
1st woman	☐
2nd man	☐
2nd woman	☐
3rd woman	☐
3rd man	☐

5.5 Prepositions – 1

This exercise gives you practice in using the right preposition together with a verb or a noun. From now on there will be an exercise of this type in each unit of the Workbook. So that you can revise these exercises later, use a pencil to fill in the gaps. Then you'll be able to erase what you wrote and do the exercise again another time.

Fill the gaps in these sentences with a suitable verb or noun + preposition from the list below.

1 In the middle of the meeting our client ...brought.. __up__ the subject of compensation.
2 All reports need to be carefully written and above all .... _____ facts.
3 The managing director was very satisfied; he .... _____ my recommendations.
4 If we want to fill the post, we'll have to .... _____ a qualified technician.
5 The clerk managed to .... _____ the two missing packages.
6 Computer operators wanted. Please .... _____ the manager within.
7 The whole company is going to .... _____ the South American order.
8 The management and the workers .... each other _____ the strike.
9 The clerks had to work long after five to deal with the .... _____ orders.
10 Our agent .... $500 _____ the fire-damaged merchandise.

account for   advertise for   apply to   approve of   backlog of   base on
benefit from   bid for   blame for   bring up ✓

Read this article and then fill each gap below with one word.

The eternal coffee break

Computers and electronic communications are allowing many people to use their homes as offices. But offices will never disappear entirely. Instead, the office of the future may become more like home

AMERICAN managers who want to get more out of their white-collar workforce will be in for a shock if they seek advice from Frank Becker, a professor at Cornell University who studies the pattern of office work. His advice: companies need to devote more office space to creating places like well-tended living rooms, where employees can sit around in comfort and chat.

Mr Becker is one of a group of academics and consultants trying to make companies more productive by linking new office technology to a better understanding of how employees work. The forecasts of a decade ago – that computers would increase office productivity, reduce white-collar payrolls and help the remaining staff to work better – have proved much too hopeful.

Mr Becker predicts that the central office will become mainly a place where workers from satellite and home-based offices meet to discuss ideas and to reaffirm their loyalty to fellow employees and the company. This will require new thoughts about the layout of office buildings. Now, spaces for copying machines, coffee rooms, meetings and reception areas usually come second to the offices in which people spend most of the day working. Mr Becker sees these common areas gradually becoming the heart of an office.

Managers, says Mr Becker, will also have to abandon their long-cherished notion that a productive employee is an employee who can be seen. Appearing on time and looking busy will soon become irrelevant. Technology and new patterns of office use will make companies judge people by what they do, not by where they spend their time.

That does not mean the end of the office, just its transformation into a social centre. New ideas about offices are catching on elsewhere. Digital Equipment Corp's subsidiary in Finland has equipped offices with reclining chairs and stuffed sofas to make them more comfortable and conducive to informal conversations and the swapping of ideas. Companies such as Apple and General Electric are experimenting along similar lines.

Steelcase, a manufacturer of office furniture, is one of the firms keenest to experiment with new office layouts and designs. The company's research centre in Grand Rapids, Michigan, is a $11m building completed in 1989. It is designed to around a series of office "neighbourhoods" that put marketing, manufacturing and design people close to each other so that they can find it easier to discuss ideas and solve problems. Employees on different floors can see one another through glass, and easily go from floor to floor via escalator.

Top managers work in a cluster of offices that are wrapped around an atrium in the middle of the building, rather than occupying the usual suite of top-floor offices. They can see, and be seen, by the people they manage.

But, sometimes even the most communicative employee just wants to be left alone.

(from *The Economist*)

1 According to Frank Becker, it is good for workers to have somewhere .... where they can sit and .... to each other.
2 Computers have .... led to an increase in office productivity.
3 A central office will be a place where off-site workers can .... for discussions and conversation.
4 Communal rooms will become the .... of an office.
5 It will no longer be desirable for workers to come to work on .... and look .... all the time.
6 Workers will be judged by what they .... not .... they spend their time.
7 Offices will become .... centres.
8 At Steelcase in Michigan workers in different .... are close to each other. And the managers are .... on the top floor.

🗣 Highlight any useful vocabulary you'd like to remember in the passage.

Ⓐ Study this summary before you do the exercises that follow.

There are different ways of speaking about past events and actions in English.

1 Talking about something **STARTING** in the past but **CONTINUING** up to the present:

> How long have you been working for the company?

> I've been here since I left school.

> Have you finished that filing?

> Yes, I've just put the last letter away.

2 Writing or saying something has happened which is **STILL RELEVANT** for the present:

We have received notification of your visit …
We have booked a room at the Plaza Hotel for the 16th March.

3 Referring to finished events that have a 'NEWS VALUE':

We've signed the contract with OBM.
Vandebrinck have at last patented their new automatic packing technique.
I've invited Jacques Lacroix over for lunch to talk about the new site plans in Le Havre.

4 Referring to events which took place **IN THE PAST**:

We dispatched the shipment, as requested.
They interviewed Roland Thoreau for the job, but he didn't get it.
Because we did a lot of advertising, we sold a lot of products last year.

5 Sometimes the ways of referring to the past can be used together:

– Have you been to the trade fair yet?
– Yes, I have. I went yesterday.
– And did you see anything worth buying?

6 Referring to events or things that happened **REGULARLY** in the past:

They used to pay their bills promptly, until the management changed.
I can still remember when there used to be typewriters in offices.

7 The past and the present can be closely related:

– Are you still working on that report?
– Yes, I am. I've been drafting a new introduction.
Mr Casagrande has travelled all over the world, but now he's working for our office in Kuala Lumpur.

B Fill the gaps in these sentences with a suitable verb from below.

1 She's ...**been trying**... to get through to head office all morning.
2 We're very busy today. The phone .... ringing since we started work this morning.
3 In 1986 our firm .... two new factories in South America.
4 I .... working here when I left school.
5 Is your secretary still looking for the file? Yes, she .... for it for the past 20 minutes.
6 While you .... lunch, Mr Casagrande called.
7 We .... the letter to the customer a week ago, but we .... a reply yet.
8 He .... in New York, but then he .... to Tokyo.

have   look   move   open   receive   send   start   stop   try ✓   work

C Look at the notes on the backgrounds of two of the export staff at Biofoods International. Then complete the sentences below.

Biofoods International, HQ, Basle, Switzerland
Export department staff for the current year

Renate: b.1964, Karlsruhe, Germany; 1984–1990
Economics and Computing, Univ. Munich; 1991
joined Biofoods as computer operator; 1993 trainee
manager; February 1995 responsible for Southern
Europe.

Pierre: b. 1950, Amiens, France; 1971–1977
electrical engineering Univ. Nantes ; 1978–1985
General Electronics San Diego, USA; 1985 joined
Biofoods France; head of Export Sales in Basle since
1989.

1 RENATE .... in 1964.
2 ....
.... from 1984 to 1990.
3 In 1991 ....
4 Since 1993 ....
5 .... since February 1995.

6 PIERRE .... in 1950.
7 From 1971 to 1977 ....
8 After this .... from 1978 to 1985.
9 In 1985 .... Biofoods.
10 .... head of Export Sales in Basle since 1989.

6 International trade

6.1 Import and export *Background information*

An import/export transaction usually requires a lot of complicated documentation. Many different arrangements have to be made and this can be difficult when one firm is dealing with another firm on the other side of the world.

Many **specialists** may be involved, including:

1 A shipping agent and/or a freight forwarder (forwarding agent) who takes responsibility for the documentation and arranges for the goods to be shipped by air, sea, rail or road. These services may also be carried out by the supplier's own export department, if they have the expertise.
2 Airlines, shipping lines, railways or road haulage firms to transport the goods.
3 Both the importer's and exporter's banks will be involved in arranging payments if a letter of credit or bill of exchange is used.
4 Customs officers who may examine the goods, check import or export licences and charge duty and/or VAT.
5 The manufacturer or a Chamber of Commerce to issue a Certificate of Origin, if this is required by the importer's country.
6 An insurance company or insurance broker to insure goods in transit.
7 An export credit insurance company (such as Hermes in Germany).
8 A lawyer if a special contract has to be drawn up.

Different **documents** may be needed, for example:
– Bill of Lading   – Dangerous Goods Note
– Sea Waybill   – Air Waybill
– Shipping Note   – Certificate of Insurance

Many of these documents can be replaced with computerized procedures. Standard 'aligned' export documentation is also used: the required information is entered on a single master document and then photocopied to produce all the required documents.

Many import or export deals are arranged through an exporter's **agent** or **distributor** abroad – in this case the importer buys from a company in his own country and this company imports the goods. Alternatively, the deal may be arranged through an importer's **buying agent** or a **buying house** acting for the importer, or through an **export house** based in the exporter's country. In this situation, the exporter sells directly to a company in his own country, who will then export the goods.

Prices for exports may be quoted in the buyer's currency, the seller's currency or in a third 'hard' currency (e.g. US dollars, Deutschmarks or Swiss Francs). The price quoted always indicates the **terms of delivery**, which conform to the international standard **Incoterms**. The terms of delivery that are most common depend on the kinds of goods being traded and the countries between which the trade is taking place.

INCOTERMS
(The most common ones are shown with *.)

CFR This price includes **Cost and Freight**, but not insurance, to a named port of destination in the buyer's country.

CIF* This price covers **Cost, Insurance and Freight** to a named port of destination in the buyer's country.

CPT The cost and transportation of the goods, **Carriage Paid** to a named destination in the buyer's country.

CIP The cost and transportation of the goods, **Carriage and Insurance Paid**, to a named destination in the buyer's country.

DAF The cost, insurance and transportation of the goods **Delivered At Frontier**.

DES The cost, insurance and transportation of the goods **Delivered Ex-Ship**.

DEQ The cost, insurance and transportation of the goods, unloaded from the ship and **Delivered Ex-Quay**.

DDU The cost, insurance and transportation of the goods **Delivered Duty Unpaid** to the buyer.

DDP The cost, insurance and transportation of the goods **Delivered Duty Paid** to the buyer.

EXW* This price is the **Ex-Works** cost of the goods. The buyer arranges collection from the supplier and pays for freight carriage and insurance.

FCA The **Free Carrier** price includes all costs to a named point of loading onto a container. The buyer pays for onward shipment and insurance.

FAS This price includes all costs to a named port of shipment **Free Alongside Ship**. The buyer pays for loading, onward shipment and insurance.

FOB* This price includes all costs of the goods **Free On Board** a ship (or aircraft) whose destination is stated in the contract. The buyer pays for onward shipment and insurance.

Methods of payment may be on a cash with order basis (or cash deposit with order), on open account (as in most domestic trade, where the buyer pays the supplier soon after receiving the goods), by irrevocable letter of credit or by bill of exchange. Exporters and importers often prefer the security of payment by confirmed irrevocable letter of credit when dealing with unknown firms in distant countries.

Trade between countries within a free trade area and within the European Union is simpler, and many firms pay for goods by cheque and use their own transport to deliver goods across frontiers. No special customs documentation is required for trade between firms in different parts of the EU, but VAT rates vary from country to country.

For more information about payment, see the Background information for Unit 7.

6.2 Documentation   *Vocabulary*

Add the missing words to the puzzle.

1 After receiving their enquiry, we sent them a ....
2 We have just received an .... for the goods we wanted.
3 Another word for 'buy' is ....
4 A bill of lading and a letter of credit are both .... used in foreign trade.
5 Please inform us when the cargo arrives at its ....

6 We send a .... before making up an order.
7 Our agents will .... the goods to you when they arrive.

8 It's important to state the .... of each package on all the forms.
9 I've just heard that .... charges are going up.
10 That firm is our sole .... of these components.
11 They have added $50 for .... and handling.
12 When will you be able to .... the goods to us?
13 The .... price is 30% higher than the wholesale price.
14 Doing business on the phone with companies .... is very costly.
15 Before we can accept your order, we require a .... of 5% of the total price.

16 When fixing a price for an export order, the .... are very important.

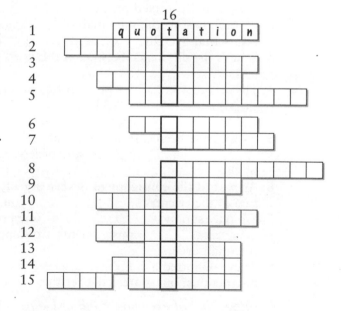

6.3 Making enquiries   *Speaking & writing* ◎◎

A ◎◎   In this exercise you'll be calling Mr Chan in Hong Kong to find the information in the list below. Speak when you hear the « *beep* » sound. Look at the example first:

Mr Chan: Hello, Orion Electronics. Thomas Chan, speaking.

« beep »
YOU: **Hello, Mr Chan, I'd like to check some information about our order number 355.**

Mr Chan: 355. Yes, what would you like to know?

« beep »
YOU: **First of all, could you tell me how many ...?**

You may need to pause the recording if you have to think before you speak.

> FIND OUT FROM ORION ELECTRONICS:
>
> 1 Number of separate consignments ....
> 2 Date of shipment of first consignment ....
> 3 Expected date of arrival here ....
> 4 Name of freight forwarders ....
> 5 And their phone number ....
> 6 Dimensions of each package ....
> 7 Weight of each package ....
>
> And tell them:
> MR FIELD will be in Hong Kong next week. He'll call to arrange a meeting.

B Draft a fax to Orion Electronics, requesting the same information. When you have done this, compare your draft with the fax in the Answer Key.

6.4 Sales and delivery   *Vocabulary*

Fill the gaps with suitable words from the list below.

1 The profits made on a product vary according to the ...**volume**... of sales and there is not normally a fixed profit .... on the unit price.
2 If you buy something by mail order it's normal to pay CWO (.....................), rather than COD (.....................).
3 What's the difference between a B/L (.....................) and a B/E (.....................)?
4 The .... price of this product at the .... (i.e. in the shops) is £13.99, incl. VAT (.....................) – about 60% more than the .... price.
5 As we have been carrying out a(n) .... control, there is a .... in processing orders. We apologize for any inconvenience caused by this ....
6 As part of the consignment is very urgent, we'll be making a .... of two of the twenty .... you have ordered.
7 We only supply .... one products of .... quality. Very .... consignments are shipped by sea. There is no .... for small orders.
8 They submitted a .... in ...., in accordance with our instructions, but it arrived after the ....

backlog   bill of exchange   bill of lading   bulky   cash on delivery   cash with order
crates   deadline   grade   hold-up   inventory (US)/stock (GB)   margin
point of sale   premium   retail   special delivery   surcharge   tender   triplicate
value added tax   volume ✓   wholesale

Look at these extracts from correspondence. What does the writer want to know in each case? The first is done for you as an example.

1 Bearing in mind the difficulties you are having with obtaining components, we were wondering whether we might expect delivery of the goods during the next two weeks or whether there is likely to be still further delay.

They want us to let them know …

a) what difficulties we are having
b) what components we are obtaining
c) when the goods will be delivered ✓

2 In view of these circumstances, may we receive your assurance that, assuming we will not be receiving the shipment before July 2, you will be prepared to offer us a discount of 10 per cent on the quoted price?

They want us to let them know if we …

a) can give them a discount
b) will ship before July 2
c) will give them a discount if shipment is delayed

3 Would you be kind enough to inform us whether the price you have quoted for the units does or does not include a twelve-month service contract, which we understood to be part of our agreement with you?

They want us to let them know …

a) if we're providing a year's free service
b) how much our service costs
c) how much the units will cost

4 We would like you to provide us with a detailed specification of the machine so that we may consult our production managers regarding the suitability of the equipment for installation in our assembly plants. Please bear in mind that the power requirements of each unit are of particular importance.

They want us to let them know …

a) if our machines are suitable for their requirements
b) if we have consulted their managers about this
c) as much as possible about the machine

5 It appears that there may have been some confusion between your quotations ER889 and ER887 and that the quantities of the former may have been inadvertently entered in the latter. We would be grateful if you could check this and inform us if an error appears to have arisen.

They want us to let them know if there is an error in our …

a) quotation ER889
b) quotation ER887
c) quotations ER889 and 887

6.6 'J.I.T.'   *Listening*

Ⓐ Before you listen to the recording, look at these 'golden rules'. Which do you think is the most efficient way of organizing a manufacturing process?

- Use your machines and workers as much as possible – they should always be working.
- Keep a good stock (inventory) of products in your warehouse so that you can supply whatever your customers demand.
- Keep a good supply of materials in your warehouse so that you never run short.
- Don't run a machine unless you are making a product that has been ordered.

B 🔊 Now listen to the recording. Here is a list of 12 points that could be made about J.I.T. – many of which you may agree with. Tick ✓ the points that are mentioned and put a cross ✗ beside the points that are not mentioned in the interview. The first is done for you as an example.

1 J.I.T. stands for 'Just in Time'. ☑
2 Capital tied up in stored materials is wasted. ☐
3 Only a large company has enough influence and muscle to introduce J.I.T. ☐
4 The J.I.T. philosophy was 'discovered' in the USA by Japanese engineers. ☐
5 Workers are laid off when there are no orders to fill. ☐
6 Some products take weeks or months to manufacture – you can't apply J.I.T. methods to such products. ☐
7 In manufacturing, materials account for about 60% of the running costs. ☐
8 Employees must be fully informed of how the system works if they are to be required to use this technology. ☐
9 Training and maintenance can be carried out if there are no orders. ☐
10 Workers have to be trained to operate many different machines. ☐
11 In bad times, suppliers have to suffer and lose money. ☐
12 Suppliers and customers have to co-operate very closely. ☐

C 🔊 Listen to the last part of the recording again and fill the gaps in this transcript. You'll need to PAUSE the recording frequently.

Interviewer: So, to come back to the supply of materials, this depends on the co-operation of your suppliers, then?

Expert: Absolutely! And changes in philosophy are essential here too. Most major companies obtain materials from over _____ different suppliers. With J.I.T. this number has to be cut down to around _____ . The benefit to the supplier is that he will get more _____ from you if he can work with you in this way. Inevitably, this involves very close _____ on the _____ and _____ of the materials he supplies and he must adopt the J.I.T. philosophy in his own _____ . If not, he'll find that the pressure is on him to hold _____ for his customers – and this will clearly not be _____ . If a supplier can't cope with J.I.T., then he'll find that major companies will simply find other suppliers who can.

D Have you changed your mind about what you thought in **A**, now that you've heard the recording?

6.7 Prepositions – 2

Fill the gaps in these sentences with a suitable word + preposition. First of all, try to do the exercise without looking at the list below.

1 I'll be ...*calling*... __*on*__ you when I'm next in town.
2 If you suffer any loss, we will .... you _____ that.
3 He was unable to .... _____ the extra work and became ill.
4 I'm afraid I can't .... _____ another department's work.
5 As you appear to have been overcharged, we will .... your account _____ the sum of ¥600,000.
6 It is important to .... _____ any special Customs regulations.
7 All members of a team must .... _____ each other.
8 We've been .... _____ our partners in the USA for several years.

9 Due to falling sales, the company has .... _____ its R & D programme.
10 They're .... _____ doing a much better job than that.
11 The cargo .... _____ four one-ton crates.
12 She couldn't .... them _____ the need to redesign the product.

call on ✓ *capable of* *collaborate with* *comment on* *compensate … for*
comply with *consist of* *convince … of* *co-operate with* *cope with*
credit … with *cut back on*

6.8 Looking into the future   *Grammar review*

A Different ways of talking or writing about future events in English have different meanings.
Study these examples:

PREDICTING future events:

> It will probably be difficult to get them to pay up on time.
> Prices will / are going to go up if the exchange rate changes.
> By this time next year, our costs will have risen by 25%.
> If the exchange rates change, prices will rise / are sure to rise.
> We'll still be unloading the goods at 3pm.
> Please don't call after 12.30, Mrs Carter will be having lunch then.

Describing a PLAN or
ARRANGEMENT:

> I'm visiting / I'll be visiting Tokyo in November.
> She's arriving / She'll be arriving this evening.

Saying what you INTEND to do:

> I'm going to chase them up if they haven't delivered by Friday.
> I'm going to have lunch early today.

Making a PROMISE:

> I'll let you know next week.
> I'll make sure Mrs Hanson calls you back as soon as she's free.
> Mr Brown will pick you up at the airport.

> My plane for Buenos Aires leaves at 14.35.
> When do you arrive in Mendoza?
> Next Friday is a public holiday in Argentina.

Referring to FACTS (timetables or schedules):

Talking about something that is going to happen VERY SOON:

> I'm just about to / just going to phone Sydney.
> They're just going to / just about to start the meeting.

It's sometimes more polite
to use *will be doing*:

> When will you be calling Mr Lee in Singapore?
> Will you be seeing Mr Kwouk while you're in Hong Kong?

instead of: *When will you call him?* or *Are you going to see him?*

Here are some common expressions that are used when referring to the future:

> *soon   without delay   before too long   in due course   as soon as possible*
> *at your earliest convenience   by return of post   in three weeks' time*

B Fill the gaps in these sentences with suitable words.

1 We   *shall be writing*   to you to confirm this when we have checked our stock position.
2 What time _____ train from Birmingham _____ ?
3 Where _____ Ms Carpenter before the conference?
4 If I _____ you before 5 pm, _____ in your office?
5 _____ me know when the goods _____ in your warehouse?
6 When _____ typing the report? I need it as soon as possible.
7 What _____ after the meeting this afternoon?
8 When _____ to ACME Industries to confirm the order?

C Fill the gaps in these sentences, using the verbs below.

1 Will you be able to find out when the first plane to Paris ...*leaves?*..
2 Tomorrow, I .... the boss for a rise and that's definite!
3 By the time I retire, I .... here for 10,000 working days.
4 She .... to Spain on Tuesday to meet our clients in Seville.
5 I .... the documents in the post to you first thing tomorrow.
6 Please don't disturb me for the next half hour, I .... Tokyo.
7 Excuse me, Mr Grey, when .... you .... to our Chinese clients?
8 While you .... in Stockholm, ... you .... Mr Olsson?
9 Stand back, everyone, he looks as if he ....!
10 Don't worry, I'm sure the spare parts .... soon.

arrive   ask   be   fly   leave ✓   phone   put   see   sneeze   work   write

D Imagine that you're talking on the phone. It's a bad line and you don't catch some of the information given, shown as ~~~. Write down the questions you'd ask.

1 We'll be able to ship the goods to you on the ~~~th of next month.
When _____ ?
2 The plane from Bombay lands here at ~~~ o'clock in the morning.
When _____ ?
3 She says she's going to apply for ~~~.
What _____ ?
4 I'll be staying here till ~~~, probably.
How long _____ ?
5 I'm leaving work this afternoon at ~~~ o'clock.
When _____ ?

E Imagine that a colleague makes a number of predictions that you disagree with. Write down what you would say to contradict him or her.

1 This will be difficult to arrange.
  ..*Oh no, it won't be difficult to arrange – it'll be easy!*..
2 Our recommendations are going to be rejected by the board.
  Oh no, they .... – ....
3 He'll still be working on his report at 5 pm.
  Oh no, ... – ....
4 Tomorrow you start work quite late, don't you?
  Oh no, ... – ....
5 I'm sure this machine is going to run reliably for a long time.
  Oh no, ... – ....

7 Money matters

7.1 Accounts and foreign payments   *Background information*

Very often in business situations you may find yourself having to talk about money with suppliers and customers. You may be physically handling money or dealing with figures and money on paper. If you work in the accounts department of a firm you may have to fill in invoices for customers' orders. Or you may have to send a customer a reminder because they have not paid an invoice. You may even have to decide whether customers can have further credit and can delay paying their outstanding bills: this is called 'credit assessment'. If you are working in international trade you may need to be familiar with the different types of payment that exist.

In most middle-sized and large firms there is an Accounts Department which deals with the money paid out to suppliers for goods delivered and the money received from customers for goods supplied.

The table below gives you a very general idea of the different activities which involve money in an accounts department. Two of the most important processes are paying suppliers and billing or controlling credit of customers. It is normal to send a *proforma* invoice in advance when supplying goods to a customer. In a situation in which the customer is known and reliable, firms may send an invoice *after* the delivery.

Accounts	dealing with money coming in and going out from a firm		
Purchasing	invoices	RECEIVE ←	from supplier
	payments – cheques, etc. (you pay the invoice)	SEND OUT →	to supplier
Sales	invoices	SEND OUT →	to supplier
	payments – cheques, etc. (you invoice the customer)	RECEIVE ←	from customer

Methods of Payment in Foreign Trade

1 **CWO – cash with order:** Note that cash simply means money in this context. This method is uncommon since you extend credit to your supplier; in addition you run the risk that the goods will not be dispatched in accordance with the contract terms. But this is usual with mail order, where you pay by Eurocheque or cheque or by using a credit card. In business,

CWO contracts often include provision for partial advance payments in the form of deposits (normally between 10 per cent and 20 per cent of the contract price). Or they include progress payments at various stages of manufacture (particularly for capital goods). Then the remainder of the payment is usually made by one of the methods described below.

2 Open account: This is a simple agreement in which you agree to pay for the goods after you have received them, usually on a monthly basis. There are various ways in which you can send money to your suppliers under open account. Your suppliers may suggest the method to be used, for example:

Cheque: This is usually the slowest method of payment. Your suppliers may have charges from their own bank and also from banks in your country since a cheque has to be cleared through the international banking system before they receive credit. Different banks have different methods and this could take as long as a month. For these reasons your suppliers may not accept payment by cheque.

Banker's draft: You can arrange for your bank to issue a draft, which is a kind of cheque, drawn on an overseas bank in either sterling or foreign currency. You send this direct to your suppliers who pay it into their bank account. Then they will usually receive immediate credit.

Telegraphic Transfer: This is the fastest method of sending money abroad but costs a little more than most other methods of transferring money. Your bank instructs an overseas bank, by cable or telex, to pay a stated amount of money to your suppliers. Your own or foreign currency may be sent in this way. If you wish, the overseas bank can be instructed to inform your suppliers as soon as the money arrives.

International Payment Order: You can arrange for your bank to instruct an overseas bank to make payment to your supplier, by airmail. International Payment Orders are slower than Telegraphic Transfers, but they are slightly cheaper because there are no cable costs.

International Money Orders: These can be purchased from your bank. You post the money order to your suppliers and they receive immediate credit from their bank in the same way as with a draft. This is a very cheap and simple way to make payment of relatively small amounts.

3 Documentary Bill of Exchange: This is a popular way of arranging payment and offers benefits for both you and your suppliers. The main advantage is that you are not required to make payment until your suppliers have dispatched the goods. Your suppliers are protected by law and also know that money owing against bills of exchange can easily be obtained. It is in effect a demand for payment from your suppliers. They will draw it up on a specially printed form or on their own headed notepaper and forward it to their bank, together with the documents relating to the transaction. These may include a transport document proving that the goods have been dispatched.

The overseas bank will send the bill and documents to a bank in your country for 'collection'. Your bank will notify you of the arrival of the documents and will pass them on to you provided that:
- if the bill is drawn 'at sight', you pay the amount of the bill in full when it is presented to you.
- if the bill is drawn payable after a certain number of days you 'accept' the bill. It means that you sign across the bill your agreement to pay the amount in full on the due date.

7.2 Financial terms *Vocabulary*

Add the missing words to the puzzle.

1 Banks .... your account when you use a Eurocheque abroad.
2 Few companies pay their shareholders a regular ....
3 .... can result if you have no more income to pay all your debts.
4 Our customers get reminders on .... payments.
5 People with large incomes or .... can always get credit from a bank.
6 Banks .... very high rates of interest on credit loans.
7 Suppliers expect their .... to be paid promptly.
8 A firm's costs include wages, interest and also ....
9 Although we have paid our bills regularly, we still have some outstanding ....
10 We hope to increase our profits for this .... year.
11 Our profits were very small despite a large ....
12 The increase in .... will not change our price policy.

13 Every year a company must allow for .... in the value of its machines and buildings.

A First you should read out each set of numbers and words below.

 On the recording you will hear someone reading out each set of numbers and words in the way in which they are spoken in English. Listen to the recording and compare it with your own reading.

1 Around £250 worth of the shares on offer
2 You can apply for 100 shares at a cost of no more than £150.
3 Sterling showed a 5 point gain at $1.3985.
4 58 x 72 cm
5 44.5 x 17 cm
6 @ DM98 per 100
7 26.8%, 47.2%, 29.9%
8 About £3.66 which works out at 19.5% per annum
9 $3\frac{1}{4}$" x $2\frac{1}{4}$"
10 $2.2 bn a year, 1,700
11 465,283
12 10.75%
13 Invoice No. R312O/SCK
14 Invoice No. 007059
15 Tel. No. 0044 533 125697

B Now you will hear someone reading out the report below. Write down the numbers in the gaps as you hear them.

Profit before tax at _____ was ahead by _____ on turnover of _____, up by _____. We must allow for the _____ review of chemists' labour and overhead costs, as well as the net impact of currency fluctuations. Adjusting for these, profits were ahead by _____ on turnover up by _____.

Retail Division turnover at _____ increased by _____, and profits at _____ were up by _____. UK sales and profits increased by _____ and _____ respectively, before property disposal surpluses.

Industrial Division achieved sales of _____, an increase of _____, with profits of _____, ahead by _____. At comparative exchange rates these increases become _____ and _____ respectively. The UK retail sales increased by _____ from an unchanged sales area.

Read this article and then fill each gap below with one word.

The CO-OPERATIVE BANK

Do *you* object to countries that deny *people* their human rights?

Help cut off the money supply from oppressive regimes

Countries that deny their citizens human rights have to get their money from somewhere if they are to survive.

But deprive them of the ability to borrow, attract international investment or process cash and they simply cannot function.

Because the hard fact is that money really does make the world go round. And stopping the money from getting to these types of countries can help exert pressure for change.

Which is why the Co-operative Bank has taken a stand. We now refuse to invest in such regimes.

With the Co-operative Bank you know you won't be supporting them

The Co-operative Bank believes a financial institution should do more than simply express concern about such countries. We believe we should actively support those involved in combating these unacceptable regimes.

Which is why our Ethical Policy clearly states that we will not invest in any country that oppresses, tortures or takes away human rights, nor will we finance the manufacture of weapons for such regimes.

And that's why all our customers know their money is not being used to back them.

Who we are – and what we stand for

The Co-operative Bank has always stood for socially responsible values since it was first formed in the early days of co-operation back in the 1870's. Our Ethical Policy was formally announced in 1992, but this was simply following our Bank's traditional outlook and values first established over 100 years ago.

In addition to refusing investment in oppressive regimes, it also makes clear:

- we will not finance companies that needlessly damage the environment
- we will not invest in businesses involved in animal experimentation for cosmetic purposes
- we will not support any organisation involved in blood sports or companies using exploitative factory farming methods
- we will not provide financial services to tobacco product manufacturers
- we will not use our finances to speculate against the pound
- we will actively seek out individuals, commercial enterprises and non-commercial organisations who have a complementary ethical stance.

Where your bank can really make a difference

Switching your current account to the the Co-operative Bank is simple.

And it won't just give you the security of knowing exactly where your money goes.

It will give us the support to challenge many accepted – but unacceptable – financial practices for the first time and exert a real pressure for change.

Time to stand up and be counted

The Co-operative Bank believes it's time to take a stand. We're making our ethical stance clear. We're making our principles plain.

If you would like to do the same, simply return this request form or phone us on 0800 828 000 to find out what you could gain by banking with us.

1 Governments which can't get money will not ....
2 The Co-operative Bank will not .... in countries with oppressive governments.
3 The Bank intends to .... people who oppose such governments.
4 The Bank was founded in the ...., but its new ethical policy wasn't made public until ....
5 The Bank refuses to invest in companies whose products it considers to be ....
6 The Bank tries to invest in companies that share its ....
7 The Bank's funds are not used to .... against the pound.
8 When you put your money in .... banks you don't know .... your money is going.

Highlight any useful vocabulary you'd like to remember in the passage.

A First read through these notes. (See **11.6** for Suffixes – 2.)

New words can be formed in English by adding suffixes.

1 Some suffixes are used to form adjectives from nouns. They usually refer to the characteristic associated with the noun they are related to.

-al   -ary   -atic   -ly

e.g.	vocation	→	vocational
	inflation	→	inflationary
	problem	→	problematic
	week	→	weekly

2 When you form adjectives from nouns the pronunciation is often slightly different.

e.g.   national /næʃənəl/ = relating to nation /neiʃən/
        disciplinary = having the features of <u>discipline</u>
        program<u>matic</u> = referring to <u>programme</u>

3 *-ish* forms adjectives from adjectives or nouns

smallish = quite small
foolish = like a fool

4 *-able* forms adjectives from verbs:

controllable = it is possible to control

B Look through these sentences and fill the gap with a word built using one of the suffixes which completes the meaning. The first one is done for you as an example.

1 The opening of the banking complex will be an important
   ...*commercial*... development for the region.   **commerce**
2 The new model was up-to-date and visually very ....   **style**
3 If you want cheap and .... products you can buy them
   at the discount supermarket.   **afford**
4 The managing director prefers to leave .... affairs to
   the accountant.   **finance**
5 The accounts department supplies us with a .... list of
   all payments.   **quarter**
6 Every company in our country is expected to contribute towards
   .... training.   **vocation**
7 The new clerk was given some .... advice about dealing
   with customers who do not pay immediately.   **caution**
8 Extra payments at Christmas are an .... feature of
   salaries in our country.   **option**
9 Before we can decide where to buy our materials we require as much
   .... information as we can get on the suppliers.   **statistics**
10 We required a .... description of all the company's
   orders since last December.   **system**

Fill each gap with the correct form of the verb, adjective or noun + preposition from the list below.

1 Company turnover has been so good that we shall be able to ...*invest*... __*in*__ some new production equipment.
2 We are one of a large number of firms which are .... _____ environmentally safe projects.
3 This uncertainty about oil prices could .... _____ our plans for expansion.
4 The accounts manager asked the auditors to .... _____ the annual figures first.
5 Our marketing department is encouraging customers to .... _____ their old machines and buy replacements.
6 If you're dealing with the French orders be sure to .... _____ the Duchamp order over all others.
7 In many countries the price of a car is .... _____ ten years' wages for a worker.
8 Most enterprises supplied by BEC .... _____ their product.
9 Our company has been .... _____ the same bank for 30 years now.
10 Our overseas customers usually .... _____ damage or loss at sea just to be safe.

deal with   dispose of   equivalent to   give priority to   have a look at
have confidence in   insure against   interfere with   invest in ✓ *involved in*

7.7 Taking a message – numbers   *Listening* ◎◎

◎◎   You'll hear four people on the phone repeating or 'reading back' from their notes the information, especially the numbers, they have just been given on some invoices. Listen to the recording as many times as you need in order to write down the information.

Listen to each section, stop the recording and fill in the relevant information in the invoice forms below. Then start the recording again. The first invoice is partly filled in for you.

1		Invoice No. **5968**
		Job Reference **177 205039**
Marks & Numbers *(not given)*		
Qty	Description	Unit Cost

3		Invoice No.
		Job Reference
Marks & Numbers		
Qty	Description	Unit Cost

2		Invoice No.
		Job Reference
Marks & Numbers		
Qty	Description	Unit Cost

4		Invoice No.
		Job Reference
Marks & Numbers		
Qty	Description	Unit Cost

A Look at these examples of what you say when you report what someone has said.

◆ Notice the verbs that are used to introduce each report.
◆ The verb in the reported part is always in the past form as are the time expressions.
◆ You normally report in the *third* person, unless you are talking about what you said yourself.

1 In statements:
'I will not come to the meeting tomorrow.'
→ She said (that) she would not come to the meeting the next day.
'This is the first bad cheque we've had this month.'
→ He said (that) that was the first bad cheque they had had that month.

2 In requests:
'Can we send you these invoices today?'
→ She asked whether she could send us those invoices the same day.
'Will you audit the figures for this year, please?'
→ They asked whether we would audit the figures for that year.

3 In questions:
'Are you seeing my colleagues next week?'
→ She wanted to know if they were seeing her colleagues the week after.
'Which of the two statements of accounts is this year's?'
→ They wanted to know which of the two statements of accounts was that year's.

B Transform the conversation below into reported speech.

1 *Anna Braun:* Good morning! I'm just calling to ask about the second quarter shipment. Has it arrived yet?
 Bill Armstrong: Well, I'm not really sure.

 ...Anna Braun called to ask whether the second quarter shipment had arrived yet....

 ...Bill Armstrong replied that he was not really sure....

2 *Anna Braun:* Do you think it could have been delayed?
 She ....

3 *Bill Armstrong:* I don't know. I have no delivery note so far.
 He ....

4 *Anna Braun:* Well, the problem is that we've no record of payment.

 ....

5 *Bill Armstrong:* And is that the reason why you are ringing today?

 ....

6 *Anna Braun:* You've always been such regular payers in the past, haven't you?

 ....

7 *Bill Armstrong:* But we have a cash-flow problem at the moment.

 ....

8 *Anna Braun:* So what do you propose we do?

 ....

9 *Bill Armstrong:* Couldn't you possibly let us have just ten days?

 ....

10 *Anna Braun:* Very well, but this will be the absolute limit.

 ....

8 Dealing with problems

8.1 Suppliers, delivery and after-sales   *Background information*

SUPPLIERS

A regular supplier, particularly if they are your sole supplier, will probably be someone whose goodwill you depend on. There may be several reasons for this:

- you may be getting a good discount from them
- you may be getting favourable terms of payment
- you may be getting extended credit from them
- they will be ready to help you out with an urgent order at short notice
- they may be working closely with you to tailor their products to your specifications
- they may be able to offer you technical advice and support whenever you need it
- you know that you can rely on them to deliver goods of the quality you require
- you know that they will deliver your orders on time

A new supplier may not be able to work with you so well and may even let you down on delivery dates – even if their prices are low and they're keen to make a good impression and get further orders from you.

DELIVERY

Goods may be shipped by air, sea, rail or road. Carriage and insurance may be:

- the supplier's responsibility – for example, with a 'CIF' (Cost, Insurance and Freight) contract, the price paid by the buyer includes shipment and insurance of the goods to an agreed point of delivery in the buyer's country.

- the buyer's responsibility – for example, with an 'ex-works' or 'ex-warehouse' contract, the buyer will arrange for the goods to be collected from the supplier's premises.
- or the responsibility may be shared – for example, with an 'FOB' (Free on Board) contract, the supplier is responsible for the goods up to the time they have been loaded on a ship, after which the buyer takes responsibility.

Goods are always insured in transit, through an insurance company or insurance brokers. Claims for damage or loss may be made if the goods have been damaged, lost or interfered with in transit. When a consignment is received, it is examined and the delivery note is signed to confirm that the goods have been received and that they are undamaged. However, damage and errors are often noticed later when the container or package is unpacked and rechecked.

Problems may be due to mistakes made by the suppliers: these can be corrected by offering the dissatisfied customer a replacement, a refund or a credit note (to be used when paying for the next order).

AFTER-SALES

A buyer's contract with a supplier often includes installation of equipment by qualified personnel, regular servicing for a limited period after delivery and having a service person on call at 24 hours' notice to fix breakdowns, etc.

Once the goods or the service have been paid for, the customers may be in a weak position because they can't refuse to pay for the goods now. Usually after-sales service is provided willingly and without argument, because it is an important aspect of marketing strategy. A company that refuses to provide good service is going to get a bad reputation, which will affect all its sales in the future. But some customers are 'professional complainers' and suppliers often have special ways of dealing with such people. Valid complaints receive more sympathetic attention!

8.2 Delays and problems   *Vocabulary*

Fill the gaps in these sentences with suitable words from the list below.

1 If any ...**merchandise**... is faulty the buyer can .... it and demand a
....

2 If the goods are damaged in ...., the suppliers may have to
.... the clients. If so, they can make an insurance ....
to recover this cost.

3 The consignment will be sent by .... on a RoRo ferry. If there is any
damage to the ...., we will offer you a .... on your
next order.

4 Our own technician·can carry out .... repairs or adjustments. But
call the suppliers' service engineer if a .... repair or
.... is required.

5 The guarantee .... last year and, unfortunately, our service contract
was not renewed and is now ....

6 Due to unforeseen ...., we couldn't clear the goods through customs,
so we paid a .... charge while they were held in a bonded
warehouse.

7 Exporters have to know about trade restrictions, such as federal or governmental
.... and ....

8 They also have to know the meaning of terms like CAD (.............................)
and d/p (.............................). The local ....
can provide useful advice to exporters.

*boycotts cash against documents Chamber of Commerce circumstances claim
compensate documents against payment expired load major merchandise ✓
minor modification quotas rebate refund reject storage transit truck/lorry
void*

Read this article and then answer the questions that follow.

Servicing manufactured goods

Take it back, son

LOS ANGELES

On June 8th the Supreme Court ordered Eastman Kodak to stand trial in a competition case about the repair of expensive photocopiers. It has thrown a spotlight on the increasingly hostile relationship in America between manufacturing companies and the firms that service and repair the goods which the manufacturers produce.

If firms chose to use an independent service company, it is alleged, Kodak refused to supply either the servicing firm or the customer with spare parts. In effect, Kodak was trying to get customers to agree not to employ any firms that competed with it for service contracts on the Kodak machines.

Many economists would side with Kodak, rather than the court. They argue that consumers take servicing costs into account when buying equipment, so restrictive service agreements are not necessarily anti-competitive as long as there is competition in the equipment market itself.

The market for servicing high-technology electronic products alone is worth roughly $100 billion a year. Thousands of independent contractors compete for the business, but the lion's share goes to equipment manufacturers.

Roughly a quarter of the revenues of America's computer makers comes from servicing and maintaining the machines they sell. Profit margins on service contracts can be as high as 50%. That comes in handy when profit margins on the sale of computers are disappearing because of recurring price wars.

Other industries may also be affected. Detroit's car makers also backed Kodak. In 1990 the retail market for car parts was worth $150 billion, about the same as that for new cars. Servicing cars came to another $100 billion on top of that. Detroit used to be happy to leave the repair business to mom-and-pop garages. No longer. Many independent distributors of spare parts complain that the big car makers are

muscling in on their business.

Big manufacturers in Japan and Germany service nearly all their own products. But America's high job mobility and entrepreneurial traditions have encouraged many engineers in high-tech industries to set up service firms of their own, often to the fury of their former employers.

Not all manufacturers are keen on the repair and service business. Makers of cheaper electronic goods, such as washing machines, televisions and video-recorders, find it cheaper and easier to replace faulty machines with new ones, or encourage customers to buy a new model, than to bother with spare parts. But many states in America require that manufacturers honour warranties on anything they sell. To satisfy the law they have appointed dealers and service agents. And yet because the manufacturers of electronic goods now view many of their products as disposable, they are in direct conflict with the dealers who have to provide service under those warranties.

(from *The Economist*)

Decide whether these statements are true (✓) or false (✗), according to the article.

1 It is alleged that Kodak refused to supply repair firms which competed with them. ☐
2 It is generally agreed that Kodak acted unfairly. ☐
3 Most servicing of electronic equipment is done by independent contractors. ☐
4 US computer manufacturers earn about half their income from selling spare parts. ☐
5 Servicing computers is more profitable than selling computers. ☐
6 US car manufacturers earn about half their income from selling spare parts. ☐
7 The number of independent servicing companies is greater in Japan and Germany than in the USA. ☐
8 If cheaper electronic products go wrong, they are more likely to be replaced than repaired. ☐

ab Highlight any useful vocabulary you'd like to remember in the passage.

Listening & note-taking ◎◎

A ◎◎ Listen to the first of two recorded telephone messages. Fill the gaps in these notes as you listen. You'll probably need to hear the message more than once.

Call from _____ Morand, _____ S.A., Bordeaux.

Both AR 707s running for 6 weeks now. Did usual routine tests before installing them
    in labs but now one unit is _____

Makes a loud harsh _____ noise, as if drive motor is
    _____ or one of the heads touching _____. Happens
    _____ times a day.

After _____ noise stopped and _____ normal.

Question: Is this a fault they should _____?

If it is a problem that needs fixing they can _____

Please confirm that this will be _____ and they can have
    _____ immediately.

Or they have unit examined by local _____ –

Call him _____ tomorrow am on _____

B Draft a short fax replying to Mr Morand, explaining what action you intend to take.

C ◎◎ Now listen to the second message and fill the gaps in these notes:

Call from _____ , _____ Electronics, Toledo, Ohio.

Re: upgrade of 4 x _____ Drives with new hardware options.

He understood we would ship them at _____, then they would upgrade
    for _____ per unit, then ship them back to us at
    _____

This arrangement was _____ in our fax to them of _____

Problems: 1 They've only received _____
           2 We've _____ their agents here for air freight and
             _____

Proposal: They will upgrade drive number _____ and
           _____ us for air freight and insurance. Please
           _____

Question: Were other 3 drives sent at the same time?

If so, maybe _____

If not, _____ at our expense.

Call him tomorrow _____ their time (_____) or send fax
    (_____).

N.B. If they don't hear from us, they'll _____ they've received and
    _____ for the upgrade!

D Draft a short fax replying to Mr Santini, explaining what action you intend to take.

Add the missing words to the puzzle.

1 This is not a serious problem, it's only a .... fault.
2 We are rejecting the goods because we consider the quality to be ....
3 If you have suffered any loss, we will of course .... you for this.
4 We intend to .... for the additional expenses we have incurred.
5 You don't need a qualified electrician to .... a computer printer.
6 A number of problems have .... since we bought the machine.
7 The delay is due to a .... of qualified staff.
8 As explained in our catalog, this program carries a 90-day ....
9 As explained in our catalogue, this programme carries a 3-month ....
10 The engineer is on call 24 hours a day if there is an ....
11 There is a lack of .... for such an old machine.
12 We must have a computer system that works well, ... of the cost.
13 Their service department is responsible for .... the machine.
14 The service contract .... all repairs to the equipment.
15 Any .... that is faulty will be returned to the supplier.

16 Please .... these faulty items.

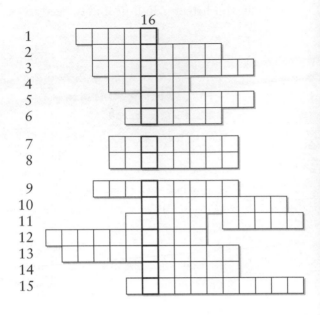

What would you say in these situations? Write down the exact words you'd use.

1 Your car wouldn't start and you have arrived a few minutes late for dinner with a client. What do you say when you arrive?
   ...I'm terribly sorry to be so late. My car wouldn't start. I hope you haven't been waiting too long....

2 Your train was delayed and you have arrived a few minutes late for lunch with some colleagues. What do you say when you arrive?
   ...Sorry I'm so late, everyone. My train was delayed....

3 You promised to call a client back yesterday but you forgot to. What do you say to him or her when you call the next day?
   ....

4 You misunderstood the instructions your boss gave you and mailed the wrong documents to your supplier.
   ....

5 You were given a copy of the sales figures by your boss, but you have mislaid it. What do you say to your boss?
   ....

6 You put the wrong date on the invoice you sent to a client. Explain why you are sending a new invoice.

....

7 You've been waiting twenty minutes for a colleague to arrive. When she appears she apologizes, using the words in Sentence 1 above. What do you reply?

....

8 Your supplier hasn't sent the correct instruction manual, in spite of your reminder to them. What do you say?

....

9 Your boss promised to call your clients in Dallas this afternoon but it's now nearly time to go home.

....

10 Ms King, a client, calls you and tells you that she thinks you have invoiced her incorrectly. What do you say?

....

8.7 Bean sticks to its back yard   *Reading*

Read this article and then fill each gap below with one word.

Bean sticks to its back yard

FREEPORT, MAINE

L.L. BEAN is a family company. Its boss, Mr Leon Gorman, is the grandson of Leon Leonwood (*sic*) Bean, the founder of America's most famous mail order business. Like Timberland, L.L. Bean first made a name for itself by making superior footwear, the famed Maine hunting boot, and has earned a deserved reputation for the quality of the $600m worth of mainly outdoor clothes and equipment it sells each year.

Mr Gorman has shown scarcely any interest in selling abroad – much like his late grandfather, who used to block suggestions that he expand markets by saying: "I'm eating three meals a day now, and I can't eat four."

So few of the 11.3m packages L.L. Bean ships each year with extraordinary dispatch and efficiency go outside North America. If the company and America's trade balance are the losers, so are the foreigners denied easy access to some of the best things made in the United States. About 94% of Bean's goods carry the L.L. Bean label, either because the product is manufactured by Bean or, as is nowadays more likely, it is made by others to its specifications. Either way, L.L. Bean stands behind all it sells.

Customers can return a Bean product for any reason at any time and they get a replacement or their money back. One recently returned a bag with bullet holes in it. In a covering note the customer explained that books in the bag had saved his life when he was hit by stray shots and could he please have a new bag. L.L. Bean said yes immediately. The company is committed to satisfying its customers, and it says it is for customers to decide whether or not they are satisfied. Foreigners have good reason to complain that they are not.

(from *The Economist*)

1 L. L. Bean is the most famous .... business in the USA.
2 It has a reputation for the .... of its products.
3 The company doesn't sell .... products abroad.
4 More of L. L. Bean's products are made by .... than by ....
5 Customers can .... any Bean product at any time and receive a .... or a .... without question.
6 L. L. Bean is committed to .... its customers.
7 The writer is .... that L. L. Bean products aren't available abroad.

ar᷾ Highlight any useful vocabulary you'd like to remember in the passage.

8.8 Prepositions – 4

Fill the gaps in these sentences with a suitable verb or noun + preposition. First try and do the exercise without looking at the list below.

1 He was ...**presented**.. __with__ a gold watch when he retired.
2 We've been .... _____ them over this since January.
3 We expect to .... a large .... _____ this deal.
4 We may have to .... _____ them to agree to our demands.
5 We have just .... _____ a new computer system _____ one of the major suppliers.
6 Unfortunately, there is a .... _____ technical information about these new processes.
7 What .... _____ our customers are completely satisfied with our product?
8 I .... _____ having to pay a handling charge to the freight forwarders.
9 Their firm has just .... _____ Apollo International.
10 Will you please .... us _____ any change to the shipping date?
11 We're .... _____ seeing your new TV advertisements.
12 I think we should .... larger quantities _____ the suppliers next month.

*lack of   look forward to   make a profit on   merge with   negotiate with
notify ... of   object to   order ... from   place an order for ... with
present ... with ✓   put pressure on   proportion of*

8.9 What if ...?   *Grammar review*

Ⓐ If you study these rules and the examples first, you'll find the exercises easier to do.

If ... sentences are used to describe or imagine the consequences of events. There are three types of conditionals:

TYPE 1 [*If ...* + present, followed by *will*] is used to imagine the consequences of events that are likely to happen or to describe the consequences of events that always happen:

> If our flight *isn't* delayed, *we'll have* lunch before the meeting.
> If you *press* the red button, the machine *will stop*.

TYPE 2 [*If ...* + past, followed by *would*] is used to imagine the consequences of events that are very unlikely to happen or events that cannot possibly happen:

> What *would you do* if you *won* a lot of money in a lottery?
> If I *was* (or *were*) in charge, I *would give* myself a rise.
> If you *placed* your hand in there, the machine *would stop* automatically.

In some situations, either Type 2 or Type 1 may be used:

> I *would go* to the USA next summer if I *could afford* to. (... but I won't be able to save up enough money)
> I'll *go* to the USA if I *manage* to save up enough money. (more optimistic)

Unit 8   Dealing with problems

TYPE 3 [*If ...* + past perfect, followed by *would have*] is used to speculate about the consequences of events that happened or began to happen in the past:

> If I *had known* this work was going to take so long, I *wouldn't have started* it before the weekend.
> If there *hadn't been* a spelling mistake in the letter of credit, the order *would have arrived* on time.

Notice the difference in meaning between *if ...* and the conjunctions in these examples:

> You can assume I'll be arriving on Thursday, *unless* you hear from me to the contrary.
>   (= if you don't hear from me)
> I'll wait here at the airport *until* she arrives.
> I'll take an overnight bag *in case* I have to stay the night.
> I'll be there to meet him *when* his plane arrives.

but notice we'd say:

> ... *if* his plane arrives before midnight.

B Fill the gaps using the verbs below:

1 If ...*I have*... enough time, ...*I'll finish*... the report tonight.
2 If the machine ...., we .... your service engineer at once.
3 If your guarantee .... still valid, any repairs .... free of charge.
4 If they .... a lower bid last month, we .... it immediately.
5 What .... you .... if you .... a colleague stealing substantial quantities of stationery from your office?
6 If you .... how angry my boss gets, you .... how nervous I feel.
7 If they .... to pay up, we .... them a threatening letter.
8 If I .... the extent of the damage, I .... all our insurance policies!

accept   be   break down   call   carry out   check   contact   do   finish ✓
foresee   have ✓   know   make   realize   refuse   see   send

C In this exercise you'll see the replies to some questions. Decide what question prompted each reply.

1 How ...*would you feel if you lost your job?*...

Lost my job? I suppose I'd feel very upset.

2 How ....?

Promoted? Oh, I'd certainly be very pleased.

3 What ....?

Work in America? I'd try to improve my English as quickly as possible.

4 Where ....?

A lot of money? I'd go on a world cruise, I think.

5 What ....?

My own company? I'd pay everyone fairly and treat them as equals.

6 What ....?

   Tomorrow? I'd stay at home and catch up on my homework.

7 What ....?

   Tomorrow? I'll wear a raincoat and take an umbrella.

8 What ....?

   Yesterday? I'd have walked to work, or gone by bike.

D Rewrite each of these sentences so that they still mean the same.

1 They expanded too quickly and they couldn't cope with the volume of orders.

   But if   *they hadn't expanded so quickly, they would have been able to cope with the volume of orders.*

2 They installed a new computer so things got worse.

   But if

3 The software was not tested and the system broke down.

   But if

4 Orders were delayed and customers complained.

   But if

5 The phone lines were overloaded and customers weren't able to get through.

   But if

6 There were a lot of problems and customers looked for a more reliable supplier.

   But if

7 Their products were excellent and many customers remained loyal.

   But if

8 The software was improved and they started to catch up on the backlog.

   But if

E Fit these conjunctions into the gaps in the sentences:

   if   in case   unless   until   when

1 We are unable to supply the goods ...**unless**... we receive payment in advance.
2 A spare axle is provided .... one is damaged during routine use.
3 The machine should not be modified .... a service engineer is present.
4 The filter should be changed .... the unit has been in operation for two months.
5 The red light will come on .... the machine overheats.
6 The machine should not be touched .... it has cooled down.
7 There's a first aid box .... someone hurts themselves.
8 The red light will not go out .... the green switch has been pressed.

9 Visitors and travellers

9.1 **Going abroad** *Vocabulary*

9.2 **Air travel in the USA** *Reading & listening*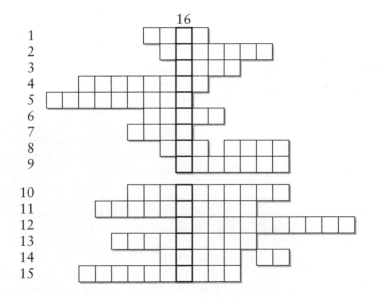

9.3 **Travelling** *Functions*

9.4 **Negative prefixes** *Word-building*

9.5 **Prepositions – 5**

9.6 **What the clever traveller knows** *Listening*

9.7 *To be* or not *to be* ... or *be -ing* ? *Grammar review*

9.1 Going abroad — *Vocabulary*

Add the missing words to the puzzle.

1 You may need a .... if you're staying in the USA for longer than a month.
2 .... class is cheaper than business or club.
3 You can .... a car at the airport.
4 You can .... to a connecting flight without reclaiming your luggage.
5 He has .... his trip to the USA till next month.
6 What is the best .... to the city centre?
7 An American asks for the check, a British person asks for the ....
8 The .... is cheaper than choosing dishes from the à la carte menu.
9 After the main course you can have a ....

10 I'm attending a .... in Geneva next month.
11 Can you get a .... to help us with this Japanese document, please?
12 Our visitor doesn't speak English, so we'll need an ....
13 How many .... will there be altogether at the congress?
14 What time do you have to .... for your flight?
15 The annual .... is held in a different city each year.

16 A charter flight is less expensive than a ....

A Before you listen to the recording, read this article and answer the questions in **B** below.

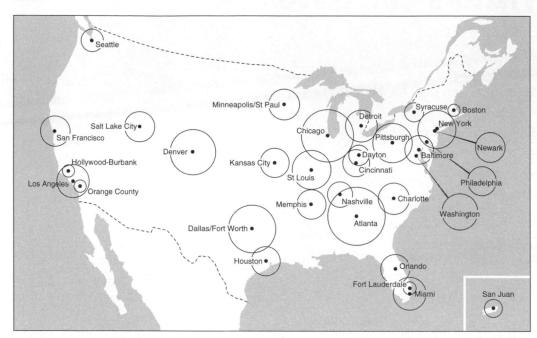

Hubs and spokes

Domestic flights in the USA are organised on the principle of hubs and spokes, like a bicycle wheel which has a hub at the centre and lots of spokes radiating out from it in all directions. One such hub is Houston in Texas: flights to over 100 other airports radiate out in different directions from there and half of these are non-stop flights.

For example, if you want to get from Miami to Los Angeles, you can catch a Continental Airlines flight from Fort Lauderdale (a few miles north of Miami and less hassle than Miami International Airport), change planes in Houston and fly on to Orange County (John Wayne Airport!) or Hollywood-Burbank Airport – both of which are much more relaxing and less crowded ways into Los Angeles than the appalling LAX (Los Angeles International Airport).

The hub and spoke network has made flights cheaper and means that even quite small places are connected to each other by a major airline or feeder service. Another advantage of the system is that connecting flights are to some extent guaranteed. If one incoming flight is up to one hour late, all the connecting flights (up to 30 or 40) will be held until it arrives. So if you're on a delayed flight, that's good news – but it's bad news for everyone else because they all have to wait for your plane to land.

From the point of view of overseas connections, many hubs also operate as entry points or 'gateways', where passengers flying in from another country can join the hub and spoke system.

The same type of system does operate in other parts of the world: for example, you can fly from one part of Europe to another via Frankfurt or Paris or Amsterdam or London, but the difference in other parts of the world is that the fares are not any cheaper so there's no special advantage.

Flying in to the USA it's advisable, if you possibly can, to avoid any major gateway, such as Los Angeles International, Miami and JFK (New York) in favour of a smaller gateway like Charlotte, Pittsburgh or Orlando.

B Using the information in the text, complete each of these sentences. The first is done for you as an example:

1 If you want to get from Miami to Los Angeles, you can …

    ....*fly from Fort Lauderdale and change planes at Houston, Texas.*...

2 If you want to avoid flying into LAX (Los Angeles International), you should …

    ....

3 If your flight is less than an hour late, your connecting flight will …

....

4 If you fly between London and Vienna via Frankfurt or Paris, instead of direct, the fare …

....

5 If you are entering the United States from abroad, you should …

....

C ◎◎ Now listen to the recording. You'll hear an interview with Nigel Isaacs, the editor of *Business Travel Weekly*. Using the information in the interview, complete each of these sentences:

1 If your flight is scheduled to take off at 5 pm, it will probably …

....

2 If you're sitting in a plane that hasn't taken off yet, you can't …

....

3 If your plane is flying round and round, waiting to land, you may feel …

....

4 If you volunteer to leave on a later flight, make sure that …

....

5 If you're travelling before a national holiday, you can expect that …

....

6 If possible, don't fly via …

....

7 If you have a small amount of luggage, don't …

....

8 If you want to be prepared for delays, take …

....

9.3 Travelling   *Functions*

Write down what you would say in each of these situations. The first is done for you as an example:

1 Your flight to Charlotte is delayed. Find out the reason.

   …*Can you tell me why there's a delay on the flight to Charlotte?*…

2 You're booked on flight LJ 879 on May 16. You want to change this to ZZ 857 on May 17.

....

3 Flight RA 372 doesn't leave till 5 pm but you've arrived at the check-in desk at 12 noon.

....

4 You don't understand how to get a ticket from an automatic machine. Ask a passer-by for help.

....

5 Someone asks you how to get to the main railway station – tell him or her that it's two blocks down and then left.

....

6 You have arrived late because your rented car wouldn't start. Apologize to your host or hostess.

....

7 You don't understand some of the dishes on the menu. Ask your companion for help.

....

8 You want to order a plain omelette, which is not on the menu.

....

9 Ask your companion to recommend a local dish.

....

10 At the end of the meal you want to pay the bill, but the waiter has given it to your companion.

....

9.4 Negative prefixes   *Word-building*

A There are many different ways of forming negative words by adding prefixes. First look at these examples:

un-	fair	unfair
dis-	like	dislike
in-	visible	invisible
non-	smoker	non-smoker

Some adjectives beginning with *l ...*, *p ...* or *r ...* form negatives like this:

il-	legal	illegal
im-	possible	impossible
ir-	regular	irregular

B Complete these columns by forming the negatives of each of the words in this list. The first ones are done for you:

accurate ✓	agree ✓	capable	certain ✓	connect
convenient	desirable	employed	experienced	foreseen
formal	fortunately	honest	known	payment
profit-making	readable	satisfied	stop	sufficient
used	valid			

un-	*dis-*	*in-*	*non-*
uncertain	disagree	inaccurate	

C Look at these examples:

anti- and **counter-** usually mean 'against':

anti-clockwise (GB) / counter-clockwise (US)
anti-freeze   anti-American

semi- means 'partly' or 'half':

a semi-skilled worker   semi-skimmed milk

Write down words that mean:

against unions .... not entirely official ....
half a circle .... not completely permanent ....
against the government .... partly automatic ....
not completely professional ....

D Now fill the gaps in these sentences, using words from the exercises above. The first is done for you as an example.

1 The claims made in this advertisement are   *dishonest.*
2 Please make sure you book me on a   flight.
3 I'm afraid the deposit you sent us was
4 Discrimination on the grounds of race, religion or sex is
5 Please inform the manager if you are in any way
6 Tourism and financial services are   exports.
7 Turn the handle   to open the door.
8 Your visa expired last week and is now
9   , your reservation didn't reach us in time.
10 Due to   circumstances, the flight has been cancelled.

9.5 Prepositions – 5

Fill the gaps in these sentences with a suitable verb or noun + preposition. The first is done for you as an example.

1 That ...*reminds*.. me __*of*__ a funny thing that once happened to me.
2 She .... _____ the firm after 25 years' service.
3 He .... _____ his post after the scandal.
4 Have you read this .... _____ the West African market?
5 We're .... _____ computer disks – I'll order some more.
6 We must achieve our targets .... _____ the amount of work we have to do.
7 He is not really .... _____ the job he has applied for.
8 Their products .... _____ paints _____ pens and stationery.
9 There has been a .... _____ the fares to the USA.
10 She is .... _____ making travel arrangements for the staff.
11 While I was abroad I nearly .... _____ money.
12 Jan and Pat both .... _____ Mr Brown, the export manager.

*qualified for   range from ... to   reduction in   regardless of   relating to
remind ... of ✓   remit money to   report on   report to   resign from   responsible for
retire from   run short of   run out of*

Ⓐ Which of these 'Tips for travellers' do you agree with? Which do you disagree with?

> Always take a good long book to read on a journey, in case of delays.
>
> Take one large suitcase — but don't pack it full.
>
> Always try to do some work on planes and trains — there are no phone calls to interrupt you.
>
> Always be very careful about local food and drink.
>
> When you're abroad treat every person you meet with respect.
>
> Do your 'homework' before you go: read books about the place you're going to, its people and their customs.

Ⓑ ◎◎ Listen to the recording. You'll hear more advice from Nigel Isaacs (the man you heard in **9.2Ⓑ**). Complete these sentences, using the information given in the interview. The first is done for you as an example.

1 You can avoid delays by …

   …only taking carry-on luggage onto a plane.…

2 You can avoid losing any important documents by keeping them …

   ....

3 You can sometimes save money flying to Australia by buying …

   ....

4 You can sometimes save money flying to Rio by buying …

   ....

5 You will need a long time to recover from a flight to Japan via …

   ....

6 You'll lose efficiency and energy by …

   ....

7 When scheduling important meetings it's wise to …

   ....

8 If you make a lot of trips abroad, it's essential to …

   ....

9 If you plan to travel with your husband or wife, it's worth …

   ....

10 You can get special facilities at a hotel by staying there regularly and …

   ....

A Study the rules and examples below and fill the gaps.

---

1 **-ing** is usually used as the **subject** of a sentence:

   Travelling abroad can be exhausting.   Meeting people can be tiring.
   _____ in a new city can be exciting.
   _____ in hotels can be lonely.
   _____ from the airport to the city is easy.

2 **-ing** is used after **prepositions**:

   Is anyone interested in playing tennis this evening?
   I'm looking forward to* _____ the USA next summer.
   I can't get used to* living in a different time zone.   *(* to is a preposition here)*
   It's unwise to travel by air without _____ a reservation.
   You can find out if flights are delayed by _____ the airport.

3 Some **verbs** are normally only used + **-ing**:

   enjoy finish dislike avoid give up don't mind practise delay ...

   I've finished reading that report.   I'm trying to give up smoking.
   I avoid _____ by car on business.
   I dislike _____ in airport lounges.
   I always enjoy _____ unusual foreign food.

4 Some **verbs** are normally only used + **to __** :

   *agree can't afford allow choose decide encourage expect forget
   help hope learn I'd like manage mean didn't mean need offer
   pretend promise recommend refuse teach train want*

   I'd like you to give me a hand with these files.
   They promised to phone me back.   He didn't mean to be rude to you.
   I can't afford _____ at the Ritz.
   We decided _____ the weekend at the seaside.
   We managed _____ two seats on tomorrow's flight.

5 Some **verbs** are used + **-ing** OR + **to __** with NO difference in meaning:

   begin continue hate intend like love prefer propose start

   She began to make/making enquiries.   I love to eat/eating Chinese food.
   She hates _____ alone in restaurants.
   Which plane do you propose _____ ?
   After the meal we continued _____

6 Some **verbs** are used + **-ing** OR + **to __** with a difference in meaning:

   stop to __ and **stop -ing**:

   Please stop making that noise, it's driving me mad!   *(= don't continue ...)*
   We stopped to get some petrol and have some lunch.   *(= stop in order to ...)*
   Their boss told them to stop _____ personal calls on the office phone.
   I was half-way through the report but I had to stop _____ the phone.

   remember to __ and **remember -ing**:

   Did you remember to call our agents in Rio yesterday?   *(= not forget ...)*
   I don't remember you asking me to, Bob.   *(= have a clear memory of ...)*
   Please remember _____ us a fax to confirm the details.
   I remember _____ her last year at the sales conference.

---

try to __ and *try -ing*:

I'm trying to open this box, but I'm just not strong enough. *(= try with difficulty or without success)*
Try hitting it with a hammer, that might work. *(= try that method)*
We tried _____ you on the phone but you weren't available.
Why didn't you try _____ me at home? You've got my number.

7 *to __* is used after some adjectives:

pleased glad surprised disappointed relieved to __

I was pleased to receive your invitation.
They were relieved to hear the plane had landed safely.
I was glad _____ my old colleague at the conference.
We were surprised _____ that the fare was over $500.

interesting kind hard essential difficult easy to __

It was interesting to see the factory.   It's hard to get a visa for Myanmar.
It's easy _____ from the airport to the city by public transport.
It was very kind of you _____ me at the station.

8 *to __* is used in these expressions: **too ... to __** and **... enough to __** :

She was clever enough to guess the answer.   My coffee is too hot to drink.
The parcel was too _____ to be sent by post.
I want to be early enough _____ a good seat on the train.

B 🔲 Highlight or underline the correct alternatives in these sentences. The first is done for you as an example.

1 **Eat / Eating / To eat**   the local food and   **drink / drinking / to drink**   the local wine made me feel ill the next morning.
2 We were very annoyed   **find out / finding out / to find out**   that customs formalities took so long.
3 I'm afraid I didn't remember   **post / posting / to post**   the letter.
4 I try   **avoid / avoiding / to avoid**   **go / going / to go**   abroad during the summer.
5 On the way to my host's house I stopped   **buy / buying / to buy**   some flowers.
6 After a long day, I was looking forward to   **have / having**   a drink, a shower and a rest.
7 If you go to live in another country it can take a long time   **get / getting / to get**   used to the way of life.
8 Have you managed   **get / getting / to get**   me a seat on tomorrow's flight?

C Fill these gaps with suitable words, using *-ing* or *to __*.

1 We'll delay ...*leaving*... until we hear the weather forecast.
2 It's essential .... a visa if you intend .... the USA.
3 Would you like .... the evening with me and my family?
4 It wasn't easy .... an interpreter who spoke both Chinese and Japanese.
5 He was talking to me about .... Japan next spring.
6 .... is not allowed in public buildings in this country.
7 There's a disco in the hotel. The music started .... at 11 pm and it stopped me .... till 3 am.
8 I tried .... a shower, but there was no hot water.
9 We agreed .... in the hotel lobby at 8 o'clock.
10 The 07.15 plane is too early for me ....
11 Thank you very much. It was very kind of you .... me.
12 Would you like me .... you a lift to the airport in my car?

10 Marketing

10.1 What is marketing?   *Background information*

Nowadays, marketing influences, and often actually controls, almost every part of a company's activities.

Underlying all marketing strategy is 'The Marketing Concept', explained here:

> THE MARKETING CONCEPT
> (We must produce what customers want, not what we want to produce)
> ↓
> This means that we PUT THE CUSTOMER FIRST
> (We organize the company so that this happens)
> ↓
> We must FIND OUT WHAT THE CUSTOMER WANTS
> (We carry out market research)
> ↓
> We must SUPPLY exactly what the customer wants
> ↓
> We can do this by offering the right MARKETING MIX: 'The Four Ps'
> = the right PRODUCT
> at the right PRICE
> available through the right channels of distribution: PLACE
> presented in the right way: PROMOTION

The Four Ps

PRODUCT = the goods or the service that you are marketing

A 'product' is not just a collection of components. A **'total product'** includes the **image** of the product, its design, quality and reliability – as well as its features and benefits. In marketing terms, political candidates and non-profit-making public services are also 'products' that people must be persuaded to 'buy' and which have to be 'presented and packaged' attractively. Products have a life-cycle, and companies are continually developing new products to replace products whose sales are declining and coming to the end of their lives.

PRICE = making it easy for the customer to buy the product

Pricing takes account of the value of a product and its quality, the ability of the customer to pay, the volume of sales required, and the prices charged by the competition. Too low a price can reduce the number of sales just as significantly as too high a price. A low price may increase sales but not as profitably as fixing a high, yet still popular, price.

As fixed costs stay fixed whatever the volume of sales, there is usually no such thing as a 'profit margin' on any single product.

PLACE = getting the product to the customer

Decisions have to be made about the channels of distribution and delivery arrangements. Retail products may go through various channels of distribution:

1 Producer → end-users (the product is sold directly to the end-user by the company's sales force, direct response advertising or direct mail (mail order))
2 Producer → retailers → end-users
3 Producer → wholesalers/agents → retailers → end-users
4 Producer → wholesalers → directly to end-users

5 Producer → multiple store groups / department stores / mail order houses → end-users

6 Producer → market → wholesalers → retailers → end-users

Each stage must add value to the product to justify the costs: the person in the middle is not normally someone who just takes their 'cut' but someone whose own sales force and delivery system can make the product available to the largest number of customers more easily and cost-effectively. One principle behind this is 'breaking down the bulk': the producer may sell in minimum quantities of, say, 10,000 to the wholesaler, who sells in minimum quantities of 100 to the retailer, who sells in minimum quantities of 1 to the end-user. A confectionery manufacturer doesn't deliver individual bars of chocolate to consumers: distribution is done through wholesalers and then retailers who each 'add value' to the product by providing a good service to their customers and stocking a wide range of similar products.

PROMOTION = presenting the product to the customer

Promotion involves the packaging and presentation of the product, its image, the product's brand name, advertising and slogans, brochures, literature, price lists, after-sales service and training, trade exhibitions or fairs, public relations, publicity and personal selling. Every product must possess a '**unique selling proposition**' (USP) – the features and benefits that make it unlike any other product in its market.

Thinking marketing

Marketing affects every aspect of a company's operations, as shown here:

> Everyone who works for the company must 'think marketing'
> ↓
> To think marketing we must have a clear idea of:
> ↓
> What the customers need
> What the customers want
> What causes them to buy
> What the product is to the customer:
> its functional, technical and economic aspects
> as well as the aesthetic, emotional and psychological aspects
> ↓
> 'FEATURES' (what the product is) + 'BENEFITS' (which means that ...)
> ↓
> We must be aware of our firm's strengths and weaknesses as well as the opportunities and threats we face in the market ('S.W.O.T.')

10.2 Ways of promoting your product   *Vocabulary*

There are many ways of attracting customers to your product and keeping your brand name in the public eye. Fill the gaps with suitable words from the list below.

1 Brochures, leaflets and catalogues can describe your product in more detail and give more information than an advertisement. Potential customers can be sent direct mail.

2 Displays in retail outlets (supermarkets, chain stores, etc.) can attract the attention of potential customers.

3 Labels and presentation increase the impact of your product.

4 You can contribute to the cost of a sporting or artistic event, where your brand name or logo is displayed prominently.

5 Potential customers can come to your premises and see a display or a demonstration of your products and get hands-on experience.

6 Your company takes a stand or mounts an exhibit to enable customers to see your products and talk to your representatives.

7 The public are informed of a new development through newspaper articles. You can inform the press by issuing press releases.

8 PR can ensure that your firm keeps a high profile, and that people are aware of your good reputation and image.

9 Existing customers tell their friends or colleagues about your product and hopefully recommend it to them.

Sales literature

10 Your staff can call customers, or customers can call a toll-free number to request sales literature or ask for information.
11 Your rep can visit customers: this is the most effective method of promotion, but also the most expensive.

Packaging   Personal selling   Point of sale advertising   Public relations   Publicity   Sales literature ✓   Showrooms   Sponsorship   Telephone sales   Trade fairs and exhibitions   Word of mouth

10.3 The story of the Swatch   *Listening*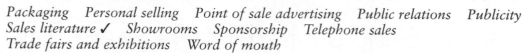

 Listen to the broadcast about the success of the Swatch. Decide whether these statements are true (✓) or false (✗).

1 Swiss luxury watch manufacturers were doing badly in the 1980s.   ☐
2 Electronic digital watches were invented in Switzerland.   ☐
3 The first digital watches were manufactured in the Far East.   ☐
4 According to market research consumers preferred analogue watches.   ☐
5 ETA developed the technology to make quartz analogue watches.   ☐
6 ETA's new product would be easy to repair.   ☐
7 Swatches would be fashion items, not timepieces.   ☐
8 In 1985 ETA spent $30 million on advertising in the USA.   ☐
9 ETA promoted Swatches by sponsoring sports.   ☐
10 There were many kinds of Swatches: some even tasted of strawberries.   ☐
11 It wasn't possible for customers to buy a Swatch at a discount.   ☐
12 ETA didn't produce as many Swatches as customers wanted.   ☐

Read this article and then fill each gap below with one word.

Are brand names being pushed off the shelf?

According to the Wall Street Journal: "More and more shoppers are by-passing household names for the cheaper, no-name products one shelf over. This shows that even the biggest and strongest brands in the world are vulnerable."

It has been clear for some time – principally since recession began to be felt in the major economies of the world – that the strength of brands has been under fire. During the second half of the eighties, the Japanese, for example, showed themselves willing to pay a huge premium to buy goods with a smart label and image to match: they were fashion victims par excellence, be it in choosing their luggage (Louis Vuitton was much favoured) or in buying their booze, where a 20-year-old version of a good malt whisky could fetch the equivalent of £60 or more. Over the past year or two, that enthusiasm to spend big money on a classy label has waned markedly.

But we may be witnessing the death of the brand.

First, every story that now appears about the troubles being experienced by makers of luxury goods triggers wise nods and told-you-so frowns.

Two days ago, LVMH in France, which owns Moët et Chandon champagne, Louis Vuitton and the Christian Lacroix fashion house, reported lower earnings for the first half of 1993 than it did a year ago. As David Jarvis, in charge of the European operations of drinks company Hiram Walker, puts it: "A few years ago, it might have been considered smart to wear a shirt with a designer's logo embroidered on the pocket; frankly, it now seems a bit naff."

This conclusion fits with one's instincts. In the straitened nineties, with nearly 3 million out of work and 425,000 people officially classed as homeless in England alone, conspicuous consumption now seems vulgar rather than chic.

But just because flashy, up-market brands have lost some of their appeal, it does not follow that all brands have done so. Cadbury's Dairy Milk is just as much a brand as Cartier watches. Tastes may have shifted downmarket, but that does not mean that they have shifted from flash-brand to no brand.

The second strand of the brand argument is tied intimately with the effects of recession. No one yet knows to what extent the apparent lack of some brands' appeal is merely a temporary phenomenon. It may well be that, deep down, we would still love to own a Louis Vuitton suitcase rather than one from Woolworth's but while we are out of work or fearing that our job is at risk, we are not prepared to express that preference by actually spending the cash.

Third, the example of Marlboro is an extreme one. The difference in price between premium brand cigarettes and budget rivals in the US had become huge during the 1980s: a packet of Marlboro or Camel might cost 80 per cent more than a budget variety. Few brands in any area of consumer goods could hope to maintain so great a premium indefinitely.

And fourth, in looking at the brands argument globally, it is too easy to become misled by what is happening in an individual market. In the UK as a whole, about one third of groceries are under supermarkets' own labels. In the USA the proportion is only 20 per cent. But it does seem that the gradual shift from manufacturer-branded to retailer-branded goods is worldwide.

As David Jarvis of Hiram Walker says: "We believe that brands will retain their halo, but people are less inclined to pay for something just because it's a fashion accessory. They need to be re-assured that the product is intrinsically better."

Reports of the death of the brand have been exaggerated. Reports of the death of the de luxe brand may be premature, but sound much more plausible.

(from *The Guardian*)

1 Consumers often prefer to buy .... unbranded products rather than more .... branded goods. The reason for this seems to be the worldwide .... in major economies.

2 In Japan consumers are less likely to buy goods with a fashionable ....

3 In the present economic climate it seems .... to spend money on expensive designer products.

4 .... brands are less popular, but .... brands are still important.

5 Maybe, when the recession is over, designer brands will regain their ....

6 In the 80s, famous-brand cigarettes cost .... per cent more than cheap brands. This difference is no longer so ....

7 In the USA proportionally .... own-label brands are sold than in Britain.

8 The consumer won't buy branded goods unless they are ....

🖦 Highlight any useful vocabulary you'd like to remember in the passage.

Add the missing words to the puzzle.

1 Please take one of these .... describing our new product.
2 There's a full description of the product on the ....
3 We are about to .... a new product.
4 You can see the trend that these figures show by looking at this ....
5 The average .... is unaware of marketing.
6 This .... shows that our sales are rising.
7 I think you'll like our new .... on the wall outside.
8 Retail outlets are being encouraged to use this window ....

9 Coca Cola and Pepsi are both famous ....
10 I think you'll agree that this new budget-price product is a real ....
11 Which of the .... should we place our advertisements in?

12 Our product compares very well with nationally advertised ....
13 According to a recent ...., 45.9% of consumers prefer not to buy imported goods.
14 The motor is exactly the same, but the case is a completely new ....
15 Which .... do our products sell best in?
16 Demand for many products may .... according to the season.
17 It's important that our .... don't find out about our new process.
18 I saw the product .... in a magazine.
19 You can buy this product in any supermarket or ....

20 Consumers must be fully aware of the .... of a product.

10.6 Prepositions – 6

Fill the gaps in these sentences with a suitable phrase from the list below. The first is done for you as an example.

1 Does anyone in the department ...**subscribe**... __to__ *The Economist*?
2 There's no point in .... money _____ radio commercials.
3 One of the factors that we should .... _____ .... is the size of the market.
4 You should .... a copy of the report _____ head office.
5 I think we should try to .... _____ our contract.
6 We believe that our product is .... _____ theirs.
7 Can I .... some of this work _____ you?
8 Their agency .... _____ public relations.
9 This guarantee seems to be .... _____ every country except ours!
10 I'll .... _____ you if you need a break.

*share ... with   specialize in   submit ... to   subscribe to ✓   superior to
take into consideration   take over from   valid for   waste ... on
withdraw from*

UK car sales by colour

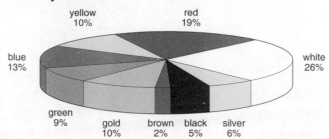

A Fill the gaps in these sentences with information from the pie chart.

1 ...**White**... is **the most popular** colour for cars in Britain.
2 .... is **the second most popular** colour for cars in Britain.
3 White cars are **20 per cent more popular** than ....
.... is **13 per cent less popular than** white.
.... **isn't as popular as** white.
4 Green cars are **not quite as popular as** .... ones.
.... cars are **a little more popular than** green ones.
5 .... cars are **just as popular as** gold ones.
6 .... seems to be **the least popular colour** for cars in Britain.
.... is **the most unpopular** colour for cars in Britain.
7 **Twice as many** yellow cars are sold **as** .... cars in Britain.
Half as many .... cars are sold **as** yellow cars.
8 **10 per cent more** red cars are sold **than** .... cars.
9 per cent **fewer** .... cars are sold **than** red ones.
Not as many .... cars are sold **as** red ones.

B 1 Each of these sentences about the bar chart contains one grammatical mistake. Find the mistakes and correct them.

1 *Canada doesn't produce as many cars ~~than~~ France.* **as**
2 *More cars are manufactured in Japan as any other country.*
3 *Much many cars are made in Germany than in Russia.*
4 *Japan is largest manufacturer of cars in the world.*
5 *3 million lesser cars are made in Spain than in Germany.*
6 *About half as many cars are produced in Italy than in France.*

World passenger car production in millions

others	2.5
Brazil	0.8
Mexico	0.8
Russia	0.9
Canada	1.0
UK	1.3
South Korea	1.3
Italy	1.5
Spain	1.8
France	3.2
Germany	4.8
USA	5.7
Japan	9.3

2 Write four more sentences:

1 The USA .... the UK.

2 South Korea .... the UK.

3 Mexico .... Germany.

4 Germany .... in the world.

C Rewrite each of these sentences, using the words given.

1 Our product is the cheapest on the market.

...*No other product on the market is as cheap as ours.*...

2 Our product is the least expensive on the market.

All the other ....

3 There are fewer competing brands on the market nowadays than ten years ago.

There aren't as many ....

4 One third of consumers prefer their product to ours.

Three times as ....

5 All other features of the product are more important than its colour.

The least ....

6 Both the price and the design are equally important to our customers.

The price is just as ....

7 Our product costs slightly less than theirs does.

Their product costs a little ....

8 Their product is nothing like as attractive as ours, we feel.

Our product is far ....

9 It's a bit more difficult to service the new model than the old one.

It isn't quite ....

10 Their product is not as reliable as ours.

Our product is ....

11 Our product is more widely available than most of the competing brands.

Most of the ....

12 Price is not as important as quality, as far as our customers are concerned.

Quality ....

11 Meetings

11.1 Different kinds of meetings   *Background information*

Business people spend quite a lot of time in meetings, and meetings come in all shapes and sizes, ranging from formal committee meetings to informal one-to-one meetings.

There are several reasons why meetings are held:

- reaching decisions in a meeting means that all the participants can feel more committed to the decision
- more information is available
- different and unexpected ideas can be contributed
- meetings can lead to more imaginative and informed decisions – often more courageous decisions than one person might feel brave enough to make

Some of the drawbacks of meetings are:

- more time is required than if one person made the decisions
- there's more talk (and this is sometimes irrelevant and repetitive)
- there's more group pressure

The larger the meeting, the longer it may take to reach a decision. There seem to be ideal sizes for meetings, depending on the purpose. A meeting where information is being given to people can be quite large, because there is not likely to be much discussion, and questions may be asked by a few individuals on everyone else's behalf.

The way a committee operates often depends on the **chairperson**: he or she may control the proceedings very strictly, or let everyone speak whenever they want. An effective chairperson should be flexible. In some committee meetings the members have to take a vote before a decision can be made: formal proposals or '**motions**' may have to be tabled, seconded and discussed before a vote can be taken. Other meetings may require a consensus of the members: everyone agrees with the decision – or at least no one disagrees.

Most meetings have an **agenda**. For a formal meeting, this document is usually circulated in advance to all participants. For an informal meeting, the agenda may be simply a list of the points that have to be dealt with. The purpose of an agenda is to speed up the meeting and keep everyone to the point. The agenda for a formal meeting must be organized in logical order. Often the agenda shows not only the topics but the meeting's function regarding each topic ('*to receive a report on ...*', '*to confirm ...*', '*to approve ...*', etc.). All items on which a decision is to be taken should appear on the agenda, which would usually have this format:

```
1 Minutes of previous meeting
2 Matters arising
3 Items
Any other business (AOB)
```

Taking **minutes**, and writing them up later, are special skills, involving decisions like '*Do we need to know which person made every point?*' and '*Is this point worth mentioning?*' Minutes usually report details of the time, date and duration of the meeting and the names of those present, but the content of the report itself may be detailed or brief, depending on the anticipated readership.

Even one-to-one or small informal meetings are structured (usually with an agenda) and planned. They are different from chance conversations in a corridor or over coffee. Small informal meetings may also take place or continue during a meal.

🔘🔘 You'll hear some extracts from a staff meeting at Rainbow Products plc. Choose the best summary of each extract below. The first is done for you as an example.

MINUTES

1 a) The consensus of the meeting was that 4,500 was a realistic target. One member disagreed.
   b) It was agreed that 4,500 was a realistic target. Mr Green stated that he was not convinced.
   c) Mr Green said the target of 4,500 was not acceptable. Ms White disagreed. ✓
2 a) Miss Grey disagreed with Mr Brown that the new product range should be marketed in the same colours as before.
   b) Mr Brown disagreed with Miss Grey that the new product range should include two new colours.
   c) It was agreed that the new product range would be marketed in the same colours as before.
3 a) Mrs Scarlet agreed to investigate the cost of employing an outside agency to prepare publicity literature.
   b) Mr Black insisted that an outside agency should be employed to prepare publicity literature.
   c) It was agreed that publicity literature prepared in-house was not of a high standard.
4 a) Ms Pink offered to draw up guidelines on the training of staff.
   b) It was agreed that staff in some sections needed training in the use of the computer.
   c) It was pointed out that Mr Gold's staff were afraid of using the computer.
5 a) Mrs Bright agreed to prepare a handout on her staff's responsibilites and send Mr Dark a copy.
   b) Mr Dark complained about the attitude of office services staff and demanded a full official description of their responsibilities.
   c) The matter of the attitude of office services staff was raised. Mrs Bright agreed to have a word with two members of her staff.

11.3 About this meeting ...   *Listening & note-taking*

You'll hear two recorded messages about this meeting:

```
Meeting on Friday 13 April
10.30 to 4.30, including lunch
Venue: Conference Room at Rainbow Products, Head Office
```

🔘🔘 Listen to the recording and make notes on the main points that are made. The first one is begun for you as an example:

To Mr Hanson	To
Ingrid Muster called from Berlin.	
Problem with flights :	

Fill the gaps in these sentences with prepositional phrases from the list below. The first is done for you as an example.

1 We shouldn't change the venue of the meeting ...**at**... such ...**short notice.**...
2 The letter we were waiting for has arrived ....
3 It wasn't done intentionally, it happened ....
4 Unfortunately, we were obliged to resell the goods ....
5 There are .... ten good reasons why we shouldn't do that.
6 As a special favour, we can supply the goods .... plus 10%.
7 Because we are clearing our stocks we can let you have the old model .... of £14.99.
8 Please reply at once ....
9 There's no hurry, you can let us know .... later in the month.
10 Please return the goods and they will be repaired ....
11 We can certainly supply you with these goods ....
12 Fortunately, we were able to resell our old equipment .... !
13 The components are being sent to Sydney .... and they'll be collected from the airport by our agent.
14 My office is .... while you're here.
15 Please send the documents to us ....

at a bargain price   at a good price   at a loss   at a profit   at cost price   at last
at least   at our expense   at short notice ✓   at your disposal   by accident   by air
by fax   by letter   by return of post/mail

Add the missing words to the puzzle.

1 Every meeting needs an ....
2 The secretary keeps the ....
3 A .... voted in favour of introducing flexible working hours.

4 A .... was passed at the meeting to approve the plans.
5 How many people are going to .... the meeting?
6 A meeting needs a .... to lead the discussion.
7 Before the main meeting we had a short .... meeting.
8 At 11.30 we decided to .... for lunch.

9 Mrs White will address the meeting on my ....
10 Let me know what the .... of the meeting is.
11 I have a .... to make.
12 A .... voted against introducing flexible working hours.
13 No one voted against – the decision was ....
14 Mr Grey has .... that we take a break for coffee.
15 There are a few more .... items to discuss.
16 Thank you very much, everyone. I think that .... our meeting.

17 But before we close the meeting: is there ....?

Ⓐ Forming personal nouns

An **advertiser** is someone who advertises.
A **supervisor** is someone who supervises people or a process.

Unfortunately, there are no easy-to-learn rules for the use of **-or** or **-er**. Here are some examples:

-er *employer adviser manager announcer treasurer*
-or *visitor administrator arbitrator competitor creditor*

❶ Now write the name of the person involved with these activities. Use a dictionary to look up any unfamiliar words.

debt	....	*invent*	....	*purchase*	....
distribute	....	*investigate*	....	*retail*	....
examine	....	*manufacture*	....	*ship*	....
inspect	....	*negotiate*	....	*supply*	....
insurer	....	*operate*	....	*wholesale*	....

❷ The counterpart of an **employer** (= someone who employs) is an **employee** (= someone who is employed). Write down the counterparts of these people:

payer ....
licensor ....
consignor ....

Note that two other suffixes are also used with similar meanings:

-ant *applicant consultant accountant immigrant attendant informant claimant participant*
-ist *machinist typist economist*

Ⓑ Forming verbs

❶ If we **summarize** something we make a summary of it.
If we **pressurize** someone, we apply pressure to them.
(In British English, these can also be spelt *summarise* and *pressurise*.)

Write down verbs that have the following meanings:

to put something in a category	to ....
to introduce computers	....
to make a state industry private	....
to make a private industry national	....
to make something legal	....
to make a general statement	....
to give a subsidy	....
to have a special knowledge	....
to make something more rational	....
to make something more modern	....

❷ If you **soften** something, you make it soft or softer.
If you **weaken** something, you make it weaker.

Write down the verbs from these adjectives:

tight loose hard bright flat sharp sweet

....

Note that we can also use the suffix **-ify** with a similar meaning:

classify qualify electrify purify simplify

Read this article and then answer the questions below.

Games people play at meetings

DO YOU ever feel as though you spend all your time in meetings?

Henry Mintzberg, in his book *The Nature of Managerial Work*, found that in large organisations managers spent 22 per cent of their time at their desk, 6 per cent on the telephone, 3 per cent on other activities, but a whopping 69 per cent in meetings.

There is a widely-held but mistaken belief that meetings are for "solving problems" and "making decisions". For a start, the number of people attending a meeting tends to be inversely proportional to their collective ability to reach conclusions and make decisions. And these are the least important elements.

Instead hours are devoted to side issues, playing elaborate games with one another. It seems, therefore, that meetings serve some purpose other than just making decisions.

All meetings have one thing in common: role-playing. The most formal role is that of chairman.

He (and it is usually a he) sets the agenda, and a good chairman will keep the meeting running on time and to the point. Sadly, the other, informal, role-players are often able to gain the upper hand. Chief is the "constant talker", who just loves to hear his or her own voice.

Then there are the "can't do" types who want to maintain the status quo. Since they have often been in the organisation for a long time, they frequently quote historical experience as a ploy to block change: "It won't work, we tried that in 1984 and it was a disaster." A more subtle version of the "can't do" type, the "yes, but . . . ", has emerged recently. They have learnt about the need to sound positive, but they still can't bear to have things change.

Another whole sub-set of characters are people who love meetings and want them to continue until 5.30pm or beyond. Irrelevant issues are their speciality. They need to call or attend meetings, either to avoid work, or

to justify their lack of performance, or simply because they do not have enough to do.

Then there are the "counter-dependents", those who usually disagree with everything that is said, particularly if it comes from the chairman or through consensus from the group. These people need to fight authority in whatever form.

Meetings can also provide attenders with a sense of identification of their status and power. In this case, managers arrange meetings as a means of communicating to others the boundaries of their exclusive club who is "in", and who is not.

A popular game is pinching someone else's suggestions. This is where someone, usually junior or female, makes an interesting suggestion early in the meeting which is not picked up. Much later, the game is played, usually by some more senior figure who propounds the idea as his own. The suggestion is of course identified with the player rather than

the initiator.

Because so many meetings end in confusion and without a decision, another more communal game is played at the end of meetings, called reaching a false consensus. Since it is important for the chairman to appear successful in problem-solving and making a decision, the group reaches a false consensus. Everyone is happy, having spent their time productively. The reality is that the decision is so ambiguous that it is never acted upon, or, if it is, there is continuing conflict, for which another meeting is necessary.

In the end, meetings provide the opportunity for social intercourse, to engage in battle in front of our bosses, to avoid unpleasant or unsatisfying work, to highlight our social status and identity. They are, in fact, a necessary though not necessarily productive psychological sideshow. Perhaps it is our civilised way of moderating, if not preventing, change.

(from *The Independent on Sunday*)

Decide whether these statements are true (✓) or false (✗), according to the article.

1 According to Henry Mintzberg, managers spend most of their working time having meetings. ☐
2 According to him, the purpose of meetings is to solve problems and make decisions. ☐
3 At a meeting every person is playing a role. ☐
4 The writer mentions eight roles that people play at meetings. ☐
5 A 'can't do' type is in favour of tradition and against new ideas. ☐
6 People who aren't invited to meetings are regarded as less important by those who do attend. ☐
7 It's normally junior people who steal other people's ideas at meetings. ☐
8 Men at meetings no longer treat women as inferiors. ☐
9 Even when no definite decisions are made at a meeting, the people often leave thinking the meeting has been useful. ☐
10 The writer believes that meetings are a waste of time and prevent changes being made. ☐

abc Highlight any useful vocabulary you'd like to remember in the passage.

A Study this information before you do the exercises that follow.

---

1 Most nouns are '**countable**':

> She's in *a meeting*.   I have *two meetings* tomorrow.
> The previous meeting lasted *an hour*.   The next meeting will last *several hours*.

And some nouns are '**uncountable**':

> I'd like *some information*.   *This information* is interesting.
> – but not: I'd like ~~an information~~.   I'd like some ~~informations~~.
>
> I have *some* good *news*.   Here's *a piece of* good *news*.   ~~The news are~~ good.
> *A piece* of new *equipment*.   *This equipment* is new.   ~~These equipments are~~ new.

Some nouns can be '**countable**' or '**uncountable**' depending on their meaning:

> I'd like *a glass* of milk.   Windows are made of *glass*.
> I'm going to buy *a paper* (a newspaper) to read.   I need *some paper* to write on.

2 *THE* is used in these cases:

Referring to things that are **unique**:

> I'm worried about *the* future.   *The* most popular brand of washing powder.
> *The* Queen of England.   *The* weather is improving, isn't it?

When it's **obvious** which one you mean:

> We're returning it to *the* suppliers.   May I use *the* phone?
> *The* meeting starts at 8 am sharp.   Have you got a copy of *the* agenda?

When we mean a **particular** person or thing:

> *The* person who chaired the meeting.   *The* problem that we have to solve is this …
> *The* manager of our Accounts Department is Ms Andrews.

And for:

> Oceans, seas & rivers: *the* Atlantic   *the* Mediterranean   *the* Mississippi
> Plural mountain groups, island groups and countries: *the* Andes
>   *the* Canary Islands   *the* Netherlands
> Hotels, cinemas, theatres, museums: *the* Ritz   *the* Gaumont   *the* Playhouse
>   *the* National Gallery

3 *A* or *AN* is used in these cases:

Referring to a **single** thing or person:

> There's *a* meeting room on every floor of the building.
> It's *an* important topic.   It was quite *an* interesting meeting.
> *A* colleague of mine.   She's *a* co-worker of Peter's.   She's such *a* shy person.

Professions or jobs:

> He's *a* personnel officer.   She's *an* engineer.

Generalizations:

> A meeting has to have *an* agenda.   A manager has to be *a* good leader.
> – or: *Meetings* have to have an agenda.   *Managers* have to be good leaders.

4 **Ø** – **no article** is used in these cases:

Generalizations about plural ideas, people or things:

> Meetings are important.   Shopkeepers are usually self-employed.
> Students don't usually have much money.

Referring to ideas that are uncountable:

> Knowledge is power.   Watching television is relaxing.
> Training is essential.   Attending meetings is exciting.

And for:

Planets, continents, countries & states: Jupiter Europe Britain California
– BUT: *the* Earth *the* Sun *the* Moon *the* USA *the* United Kingdom
Languages: English Dutch Thai
Mountains and lakes: Mount Fuji Lake Superior
Streets, roads & squares: Oxford Street Madison Avenue Trafalgar Square
Parks, stations & public buildings: Hyde Park Grand Central Station
    Heathrow Airport

⚠ NOTE: All the above rules are just 'rules of thumb' – you may be able to think of some exceptions, and you'll come across more exceptions.

Ⓑ Find the mistakes in these sentences and correct them. Each sentence contains TWO mistakes!

1 ~~The~~ most people agree that ~~the~~ women can do the same work as men.
2 The trouble with the large meetings is that they go on for longer time than small ones.
3 You have to catch train from the Paddington Station to get to Wales.
4 She's a student and she's studying the economics at the Vienna Technical University.
5 I'm staying in the room number 609 at Holiday Inn near the airport.
6 The most of my colleagues are more interested in the sport than in business.
7 Could you give me an information about the venue of meeting?
8 Does the machine need new component or do we need to think about ordering a new equipment?
9 I sometimes get feeling that I spend all my time in the meetings.
10 I don't enjoy talking on a phone, I prefer to send a fax or write the letters.

Ⓒ Fill the gaps in these paragraphs with **a**, **an**, **one**, **the** or **0** (no article):

1 More and more,   shoppers are by-passing   household names for   cheaper no-name products   shelf over. This shows that even   biggest and strongest brands in   world are vulnerable.

2   larger   meeting,   longer it may take to reach   decision. There seem to be   ideal sizes for   meetings, depending on   purpose.   meeting where   information is being given to   people can be quite large, because there is not likely to be much discussion, and   questions may be asked by   few individuals on everyone else's behalf.

3 Even   one-to-one or   small informal meetings are structured (usually with   agenda) and planned. They are different from   chance conversations in   corridor or over   coffee.   small informal meetings may also take place or continue during   meal.

4 All   meetings have   thing in   common: role-playing.   most formal role is that of   chairman. He (and it is usually   he) sets   agenda, and   good chairman will keep   meeting running on   time and to   point. Sadly,   other, informal role-players are often able to gain   upper hand. Chief is   "constant talker", who just loves to hear his or her own voice.

12 Processes and operations

12.1 How things work   *Background information*

Operations: Explaining how things work

Describing how things function in a non-technical fashion is frequently required in business. You may have to explain how to operate a machine like a computer or an automatic ticket machine, or how to use a gadget. Also you'll need to understand explanations of how to get machines or gadgets to work.

It's important to be able to adjust your language in order to take into account the people you're talking to, whether they are your customers, clients or colleagues. People who use modern machines aren't all experts who understand the technical processes and terms. To be user-friendly you'll need to employ simple instructions in language which isn't too technical. After all, you'll often be dealing with non-experts, and they may not know the difficult words, so you'll have to explain them.

Describing commercial and manufacturing processes

You may have to describe commercial processes and tell others how things are done. Business operations are becoming increasingly more complex, and some parts of business deals may involve explaining specific arrangements or processes in a simplified way.

Perhaps you'll have to describe how a manufacturing process is organized, or you may have to explain the details of services which are offered and how they're arranged. You'll need to explain when certain things happen and in what order. In addition, in some business settings, when things don't go according to plan you may be required to refer to and clarify problems that arise in the course of a production process or commercial operation.

'Technological' processes may be involved. These frequently take place on production lines, in factories or in workshops, where raw materials are transformed into finished products. In many countries the use of machines has long been associated with manufacturing goods. Increasingly, such processes are being partly and even fully automated. Robots may be used to replace people in dangerous and unhealthy or boring and repetitive tasks. But people are always required in manufacturing, in maintaining the robots, for example. So it's practically impossible to deal with technical processes without considering the role that people involved in the business operations play. So, given the rate of change in industry and commerce, it's quite likely that business people may be expected to refer to fairly complex manufacturing processes and operations, even if they aren't involved in them on a day-to-day basis.

Add the missing words to the puzzle.

1 A well planned and organized operation will help to .... and make easier the achievement of commercial objectives.

2 Be careful to .... the batteries the right way round or else the device will not work.

3 Before you assemble a table you need to .... all the parts in the right place.

4 New Zealand's main .... are good agricultural land, forests and water power.

5 To make the operation more simple and more effective we shall have to .... staff employed.

6 Despite a large number of problems and .... the prototype came out on schedule.

7 In order to clean and service the machine you need to .... it and then put it back together again.

8 In the course of refining oil, gas is a major ....-.... which arises and is not always needed.

9 We shall need to .... the specifications slightly for the Czech market.

10 When the machines stop running the engineers have the opportunity to carry out the necessary ....

11 Before you can manufacture the heavy-duty batteries, you'll have to .... your capacity.

12 The union is worried about the plans to cut back .... in the new plant.

13 The majority of car manufacturers still produce their vehicles on an ....

Numbered clue positions: 1, 2, 3, 4, 5, 6, 7, 8, 9, 10, 11, 12

13 f a c i l i t a t e

Before you do this exercise look at the expressions in **12.2B** in the Student's Book.

A Write down what you would say in these situations. The first is done for you as an example.

What would you say ...

1 when you explain to someone you know fairly well how to switch a computer on?

 ....'OK, now first of all, you switch it on by pressing this key.'....

2 when you are showing someone you know fairly well which button to press on a machine?

 ....

3 when you want to check that the other person understands what you've just explained?

 ....

4 if you want to add a further point to your explanation?

 ....

5 when you want to ask a stranger to help you use a photocopier which you don't know how to use?

 ....

6 when you want to ask a friend to show you how a machine works?

....

7 if you need a further explanation?

....

8 when you think you've understood what a friend has said but you want them to repeat it?

....

B ◎◎ Listen to the recording. You'll hear four people explaining how to use something or how to carry out an operation. Listen and decide what it is that is being explained.

1 ....

2 ....

3 ....

4 ....

12.4 In ...   *Prepositional phrases – 2*

Fill the gaps in these sentences with a suitable prepositional phrase from the list below.

1 Could you please remain ...*in contact with*... the head office until the negotiations are completed?

2 As long as the talks are .... the negotiating committee will say nothing to the press.

3 We are forwarding all the items on the list .... your request.

4 Most companies only deliver such items ...., as it is cheaper in the long run.

5 We have to request payment .... for all orders under $100.

6 We must ask you to take full responsibility for the goods, as long as they are

....

7 Our local agent will then make a final decision .... the regional director.

8 We must ask you to treat this information .... until the report is finally published.

9 Ms Andreotti has been .... our Rome sales office since last year.

10 Although the partners were ...., they succeeded in paying our bill.

in accordance with   in advance   in bulk   in charge of   in confidence
in consultation with   in contact with ✓   in debt   in progress   in transit

You'll hear an interview with an expert discussing a technique which is being developed to 'reduce' noise both in the working environment and outside it.

A ◎◎ Listen to the interview and decide which of these statements best describes how the technique which is discussed works.

☐ Anti-noise removes other noises.
☐ Anti-noise uses the technique of 'muffling'.
☐ Anti-noise creates vibrations which affect sound waves.

B ◎◎ Listen to the interview again and answer these questions:

1 The expert says that …
   a) the technology to make machines quieter has been available since the 1930s.
   b) the method for making machines quieter has only recently been developed.
   c) the technology for quietening machines has only now become commercially possible.

2 According to the expert, American industry …
   a) is paying millions to compensate their customers for noise.
   b) passes on the costs of noise to their customers.
   c) does not follow the regulations because they are too expensive.

3 Current techniques used to dampen down noise and vibration …
   a) are thirty or forty years old.
   b) can result in the efficient performance of mufflers.
   c) cause noisy components to suffer.

4 The expert claims that the new systems can …
   a) deal with repetitive noise.
   b) eliminate noise completely.
   c) deal with one-off noise.

5 The expert describes a new technique using a microphone and a microprocessor which …
   a) responds to particular types of noise.
   b) produces noise quieter than the car engine.
   c) causes the car engine to run more quietly.

6 The expert refers to one area of application which …
   a) cannot minimize the noise of aircraft engines and helicopter vibrations.
   b) would be able to reduce noise in the cabin of an aircraft to more acceptable levels.
   c) has resulted in new aircraft engines that are noisier than earlier ones.

7 According to the expert, people working in loud workplaces with anti-noise systems …
   a) are affected by the effects of noise.
   b) can work more efficiently in 'zones of quiet'.
   c) can hear conversations from another part of the room.

Read this article and then fill each gap below with one word.

About time

For the manager of the 1990s, time is apparently of the essence. Consumers, the argument runs, want to get their hands on the products – be they burgers or Buicks – faster than ever. The fashionable will buy from your firm only if you have the latest designs before your rivals. Better still, they will invariably pay more for the privilege of speed.

The key is to look at the entire manufacturing operation and then restructure that, systematically.

Traditionally, manufacturing is a carefully ordered affair: tasks usually have a sequence that can be changed only in small ways. Most firms will have employed specialists to determine the best scheduling logic for manufacturing. But "precedence constraints" (eg task A must be carried out before task B) can cause queues and bottlenecks in even the most logical manufacturing process. This not only results in delay, it also introduces an unpredictable variability into a company's operations.

There is a cheaper route. By breaking down tasks into ever smaller, faster bits, companies can increase their manufacturing flexibility. This, in turn, will tend to increase the number of tasks that can be performed in parallel rather than in sequence. For instance, several smaller machines can be used to perform one task, rather than a single large machine. Parallel tasks have no precedence constraints and can reduce bottlenecks. That helps speed a company's manufacturing process closer to the theoretical ideal – which reduces queues and bottlenecks elsewhere in the factory.

Perhaps the single most effective answer to the problem is to invest in lots of excess capacity. It eliminates queuing and bottlenecks, sharply reducing unpredictable variations in the time needed to complete each part of the manufacturing process. As a consequence, production times tend to fall while manufacturing reliability (and hence the reliability of products) soars. It also introduces much greater flexibility into the factory – which helps companies respond more rapidly to customers' whims.

All told, experts reckon that cutting production times by a quarter can reduce overall costs by about a fifth.

If it sounds too costly and risky, concentrate on the margin. Benetton, an Italian clothes company, does just that, as does Nissan. For the core products bought by the bulk of their customers, a prompt response to new trends is not a priority. But for their growing number of faddish, innovation-loving customers, these companies have developed fast-response marketing, manufacturing and distribution. Benetton has undyed stocks of clothes waiting to be coloured according to the latest trends. Nissan will quickly assemble from standardised components a limited run of vehicles for micro-niches in the market – including speciality versions of its snail-like S-Cargo delivery vans suitably tailored for customers such as bakeries, flower shops or boutiques.

(from *The Economist*)

1 Consumers will pay .... for goods if they can get them ....
2 Manufacturing operations are broken into small .... which have to happen in a particular ....
3 .... or .... may occur which hold up the process.
4 Manufacturers can become more .... if more tasks are performed in parallel.
5 Several .... machines are better than one .... machine.
6 If manufacturers .... in increased capacity, they can .... to customers' requirements more quickly.
7 Benetton can respond quickly to changes in ....
8 Nissan uses .... components to assemble limited .... of vehicles that only a few people want.

ar Highlight any useful vocabulary you'd like to remember in the passage.

Ⓐ Look at the different uses of these modal verbs.

Possibility

1 When you say something **may** or **might** happen or be true, it will **possibly** happen or be true in the future, but is not certain:

> Carol *may* finish it by tonight.
> Things change, I *might* even lose my job.

2 **Can** is used to indicate that it is **possible** for someone to do something or for something to happen:

> Anybody *can* learn how to use a keyboard.

3 You use **could** to indicate that you think that something is **possibly true** or is a possible explanation for something:

> That *could* be one reason why it broke.

4 **Could** is also used with *I* and *we* to indicate that something is **possible** and that you are considering doing it:

> I *could* ask him to help, I suppose.
> We *could* send the part on Friday.

5 You also use **might** when you give **advice** or suggest something:

> There are a few things we *might* compare notes on.

6 **Could** is also used (usually with *you*) to make a **suggestion**:

> *Couldn't* you just employ more staff to finish the order?

7 **Can** is also used to say that something is **allowed**:

> What are the rules for when you *can* and *can't* go on holiday?

8 **May** is used in questions to ask for **permission**:

> *May* I look around the plant now?

Obligation

9 If you say that someone **must** or **must not** do something, you think it is **very important** for them to do it or not to do it:

> You *must* learn to remain calm under pressure.
> You *must not* use the machine until the green light is on.

10 You tell someone that they **have to** do something when you are giving them an **instruction** or telling them how to act:

> You *have to* watch the control lamp before using the machine.
> She'll *have to* spend a lot of money if she wants the new model.

11 **Have got to** is an informal way of saying *must* or *have to*:

> If you want to finish early, you*'ve got* to concentrate very hard now.
> We*'ve* all *got* to work together on this project.

12 You use **should** or **ought to** to say that you think it is **a good idea** and important for something to be done, and that it would be slightly wrong not to do it:

> *Shouldn't* you switch that off first?
> *Oughtn't* we *to* phone for the police?
> We *ought to* order a replacement, oughtn't we?

13 You use **ought to** or **should** to say that you think that an action or someone else's behaviour is morally **right**:

> They *ought to* earn more money for all their effort.
> Somebody *ought to* do something about it.

14 When you say something *need not* happen, you mean that it **might** happen but that it is **not necessary** that it will happen:

Such tax cuts *need not* be inflationary.
It *needn't* cost very much to produce.

15 If you tell someone *they* must do something, you are **suggesting** that they should do it or **inviting** them to do it:

You *must* call on me at the office, when you're here.
You *must* come round for a meal some time.

B Rewrite each of the sentences starting with the words given and using one of the modal verbs. The first one is done for you as an example.

1 The Swedish company will possibly buy our company.
   ...The Swedish company might buy our company....

2 It's possible for the firm to build the car at this plant.
   The firm ....

3 It is possible that is why the company closed down.
   That ....

4 We are considering enlarging the present site.
   We ....

5 The workforce is allowed to use this canteen.
   They ....

6 It is very important to follow the instructions closely.
   You ....

7 I think it is right for the company to pay more for overtime.
   They ....

8 It is not necessary for the assembly line to stop for them to do the maintenance work.
   The assembly line ....

9 Experience is essential for this job.
   You ....

10 We're not able to help you this time.
   We ....

C Look at this set of sentences containing modal verbs. Match each sentence with a sentence on the right which means the same. The first one has been done as an example.

1 We can't do it free. —————————————— a) We're not able to do it free.
2 Couldn't the engine be repaired before
   the end of the week?
3 Regular customers oughtn't to wait for
   their service visits.
4 I might finish the job if I work
   overtime tonight.
5 We could open the new department on
   the first of the month.
6 We need a fully automated assembly
   line if we want to compete on the
   world market.
7 The plane might be late.
8 The travel agent should refund the ticket.

b) Perhaps the plane will be late.
c) It is possible for us to open the new
   department on the first of the month.
d) Isn't it possible to repair the engine
   before the end of the week?
e) Perhaps I'll be able to finish the job if
   I work overtime tonight.
f) It's not right for regular customers to
   wait for their service visits.
g) It's right for the travel agent to refund
   the ticket.
h) It's essential to have a fully automated
   assembly line if we want to compete
   on the world market.

13 Jobs and careers

13.1 Applications and interviews   *Background information*

In different countries, different conventions apply to the process of job application and interviews. In most parts of the world, it's common to submit a typed or laser-printed CV (curriculum vitae – British English) or résumé (American English). This contains all the unchanging information about you: your education, background and work experience. This usually accompanies a letter of application, which in some countries is expected to be handwritten, not word-processed. A supplementary information sheet containing information relevant to this particular job may also be required, though this is not used in some countries.

Many companies expect all your personal information to be entered on a standard application form. Unfortunately, no two application forms are alike, and filling in each one may present unexpected difficulties. Some personnel departments believe that the CV and application letter give a better impression of a candidate than a form.

There are different kinds of interviews: traditional one-to-one interviews, panel interviews where one or more candidates are interviewed by a panel of interviewers and even 'deep-end' interviews where applicants have to demonstrate how they can cope in actual business situations. The atmosphere of an interview may vary from the informal to the formal and interviewers may take a friendly, neutral or even hostile approach. Different interviewers use different techniques and the only rules that applicants should be aware of may be '*Expect the unexpected*' and '*Be yourself*'!

Progress interviews are interviews where employees have a chance to review the work they are doing and to set objectives for the future. Such interviews usually take place after a new employee has been working with a company for several months, and after that they may take place once or twice a year.

In different countries, and in different trades and different grades, the salary that goes with a job may be only part of the package: extra benefits like a company car or cheap housing loans, bonuses paid in a 'thirteenth month', company pension schemes, free canteen meals, long holidays or flexible working hours may all contribute to the attractiveness of a job.

A Before you listen to the recording, look at this advertisement and decide what kind of person the advertiser is looking for. Highlight the important points in the ad.

> ## Assistant Marketing Manager
>
> We are a well-known international manufacturer, based in the UK, and we are expanding our export marketing activities in our European headquarters in London.
>
> We are looking for a lively and intelligent person to join our team as soon as possible.
>
> The work will involve working in our London office, telephoning and corresponding with our overseas clients and agents, and some travel, mainly to European countries. Applicants should be fluent in at least one foreign language. Experience in marketing would be an asset but not essential.
>
> The successful applicant will be paid top London rates and provided with generous removal expenses.

B You'll hear three telephone messages. Each of the speakers has held interviews with applicants for the job.

1 Listen and take notes. You'll need to pause the recording frequently.

2 Compare your notes with the notes in the Answer Key.

3 Decide which of the job applicants sounds most promising:
Which of them will you put on the short list for a second interview in London?
Which of the three candidates do you rate most highly, judging from what you've heard about them?

➡ If possible, compare your views with another student who has done this exercise.

```
REPORT FROM:


Best candidate: ..................................................  Age: ..........
Education: ...............................................................................
Languages: ...............................................................................
Work experience: ......................................................................
............................................................................................
Personality: .............................................................................
............................................................................................
Availability: .............................................................................
Suitability: ..............................................................................
............................................................................................
Address: ..................................................................................
Phone: ....................................................................................
```

Use a dictionary to look up any unfamiliar words in these exercises.

A Verbs → nouns

1 Abstract nouns can be formed from many verbs by adding **-ment** or **-tion**. Look at these examples:

-ment		**-tion**	
manage	management	connect	connection
improve	improvement	classify	classification
		duplicate	duplication
		educate	education

2 What are the noun forms of these verbs? Only write down the ones which are unfamiliar or which you're unsure of.

*acknowledge   achieve   agree   announce   arrange   develop   endorse   judge
    measure   repay*

*adapt   alter   apply   authorize   cancel   centralize   confirm   consult   declare
    determine   devalue   imagine   modify   recommend   specialize*

*appreciate   arbitrate   calculate   collaborate   co-operate   eliminate   fluctuate
    integrate   locate   speculate*

*attract   collect   contribute   correct   deduct   delete   interrupt   pollute
    predict   protect   reduce*

3 Abstract nouns are formed from some verbs by adding **-al** or **-ance**. Look at these examples:

-al		**-ance**	
arrive	arrival	accept	acceptance
withdraw	withdrawal	appear	appearance
refuse	refusal	assist	assistance
		perform	performance

B Adjectives → nouns

1 Nouns can be formed from adjectives by adding **-ness**, **-ence** or **-ity**. Look at these examples:

-ness		**-ence**		**-ity**	
aware	awareness	negligent	negligence	able	ability
bright	brightness	insistent	insistence	available	availability

2 What are the noun forms of these adjectives? Only write down the ones which are unfamiliar or which you're unsure of.

calm   careless   cheap   friendly   helpful   late   loud   serious

confident   intelligent   patient   different

*capable   flexible   formal   possible   probable   popular   real   reliable   scarce
sincere*

Read this article and then fill each gap below with one word.

Employee loyalty in service firms

Have a nice day

NEW YORK

Hotel, shop and restaurant chains, which employ thousands of people in low-paid, dead-end jobs, are discovering that high labour turnover rates resulting from the indiscriminate hiring of "cheap" workers can be extremely costly.

Cole National, a Cleveland-based firm which owns Child World, Things Remembered and other speciality shops, declared a "war for people" in an effort to recruit and keep better staff.

Employees were asked: What do you enjoy about working here? In the past year, have you thought about leaving? If so, why? How can we improve our company and create an even better place to work? Employees replied they wanted better training, better communications with their supervisors and, above all, wanted their bosses to "make me feel like I make a difference". Labour turnover declined by more than half; for full time sales assistants, it declined by about a third.

Marriott Corporation, a hotels and restaurants group, has also decided to spend more money on retaining employees in the hope of spending less on finding and training new ones. In one year, it had to hire no fewer than 27,000 workers to fill 8,800 hourly-paid job slots.

To slow its labour turnover, Marriott had to get a simple message accepted throughout its operating divisions: loyal, well motivated employees make customers happy and that, in turn, creates fatter profits and happier shareholders. Improved training of middle managers helped. So did a change in bonus arrangements.

At the same time, Marriott became more fussy about the people it recruited. It screened out job applicants motivated mainly by money: applicants which the company pejoratively described as "pay first people". Such people form a surprisingly small, though apparently disruptive, part of the service-industry workforce. Marriott found in its employee-attitude surveys that only about 20% of its workers at Roy Rogers restaurants and about 30% of its workers at Marriott hotels regarded pay as their primary reason for working there.

Many middle managers in service industries are more comfortable coping with demands for more money than with demands for increased recognition and better communications. They will have to change their ways. Surveys say that when 13,000 employees in retail shops across America were asked to list in order the 18 reasons for working where they did, they ranked "good pay" third. In first place was "appreciation of work done", with "respect for me as a person" second.

(from *The Economist*)

1 Many workers in service industries are .... badly and their work is ....

2 Service firms with large numbers of low-paid workers often have a high staff ....

3 Cole National conducted a .... among its staff, because they wanted to recruit and .... better workers.

4 Staff replied that they wanted their managers to show that they were ....

5 Marriott discovered that customers are happier when the staff are .... and .... motivated. They found that most of their workers were .... mainly motivated by pay.

6 For most US shop workers pay is the .... most important reason for job satisfaction.

▮▮ Highlight any useful vocabulary you'd like to remember in the passage.

13.5 Employment   *Vocabulary*

Fill the gaps in these sentences, then add the words to the puzzle below.

1 In American English, you .... an application form.
2 She's going to make engineering her ....
3 Are we going to .... a new sales manager?
4 He was the most promising .... for the job.
5 The past tense of *seek* is ....
6 All our production workers are paid top ....
7 The applicants will be interviewed by the .... of directors.
8 Mr and Mrs Smith supplement their .... by renting out rooms.
9 A well-prepared .... will do well at any interview.
10 The applicants were interviewed by a .... of three managers.
11 If you're ....-.... you're your own boss.
12 Could you explain to me what the .... of the job are?
13 How much .... will I have to pay?
14 What is your present annual ....?

15 A company car, subsidized meals or low-interest loans are all ....

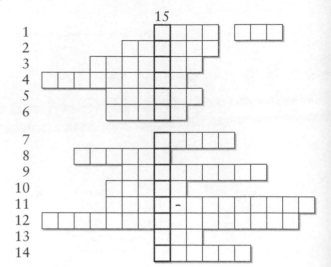

13.6 On ...   *Prepositional phrases – 3*

Fill the gaps in these sentences with a suitable prepositional phrase from the list below.

1 They produce this kind of material ...*on a large scale*... so they should be able to supply us quickly.
2 You will find our new product .... at our showroom.
3 We have a sales engineer .... who can fix the fault this week.
4 We can supply samples and demonstration equipment ....
5 We have had the goods .... for three months, but they haven't arrived yet.
6 We accepted delivery of the goods as undamaged, but .... we find that five of the components are unusable.
7 I spoke to him .... last week about this.
8 We can have the goods for four weeks .... Then we can return them or pay for them.
9 The goods arrived ....
10 He travelled to England .... but managed to do a little sightseeing while he was there.
11 I'm afraid Ms Smith is .... till the end of the month – can I help you?
12 We can offer you the job .... that you start work on the first of next month.
13 This candidate doesn't look very good .... but she is very impressive in person.
14 You can't keep this permanently, but you may have it .... till the end of the month.
15 She signed the letter .... her boss.
16 Our relocation plans are proceeding .... and we will be making the move on January 1 next year.

on a large scale ✓   *on approval   on behalf of   on business   on closer inspection*
on condition   on display   on loan   on order   on paper   on the phone   on request   on schedule
on the spot   on time   on vacation / on holiday

You'll hear part of a broadcast about high-flyers – people who will be given special training and experience to make them into the top managers of tomorrow. Answer these multiple-choice questions about the information and opinions given in the recording.

According to the Presenter ...

1 High-flyer schemes are ...
   a) found in all kinds of companies.
   b) most common in multinational companies.
   c) common in large companies.
2 In a large company ...
   a) only a high-flyer can climb the promotion ladder more quickly.
   b) a bright person can quickly climb the promotion ladder even if there is no high-flyer scheme.
   c) the career structure is normally quite flexible.
3 A member of a high-flyer scheme will ...
   a) obtain wide experience in different departments.
   b) already have wide experience in different fields.
   c) become a specialist in his or her chosen field.

According to Rod Scott ...

4 BP ...
   a) is the world's largest multinational company.
   b) has about 130,000 employees worldwide.
   c) has about 130,000 employees in the UK.
5 There are .... people participating in BP's 'individual development programme'.
   a) 130   b) 180   c) 260
6 BP's high-flyers join the scheme when ...
   a) they have just joined the group.
   b) they have been with the group for ten years.
   c) they have already shown their potential.

According to Heather Stewart ...

7 A high-flyer scheme may ...
   a) produce a management team who can work well together.
   b) lead to a lack of flexibility in the management team.
   c) prevent the business from changing.
8 A company with a high-flyer scheme tends ...
   a) to be less competitive.
   b) not to recruit senior staff from outside the company.
   c) to lose good managers, who leave to join their competitors.
9 High-flyer schemes tend not to recognize the importance of ...
   a) academic qualifications.
   b) people who join the company later.
   c) the experience and knowledge of older people.
10 Women managers are excluded from high-flyer schemes because ...
   a) they are expected to leave to have babies.
   b) they prefer to have babies instead of a career.
   c) this is the age they are most likely to have babies.
11 Other able, enthusiastic managers ...
   a) consider high-flyers to be better than them.
   b) lose their motivation.
   c) leave the company if they aren't selected as high-flyers.
12 In medium-size companies high-flyer schemes ...
   a) are usually experimental.
   b) are unpopular.
   c) are unnecessary because the career structure is flexible.

(A) Study these rules and examples before you start the exercises.

There are two types of relative clause in English:

1 Identifying relative clauses identify a person or thing in the same sentence. Notice the lack of commas:

> You seem a bit upset – why is that?
> – Well, you see, I applied for a job *that I saw advertised last month*.
> But you didn't get it?
> – No, I phoned first and then I wrote a long letter. And the letter *that I got back* was just a photocopy! It said that the job *that I wanted* had already been given to someone inside the company.
> But you thought that it was still vacant?
> – Yes, the person *who spoke to me on the phone* told me the post was vacant.
> How annoying!

Instead of **that** we can use **which** – and instead of **who** we can use **that**. If, and only if, the subordinate clause (in italics in the examples) has a subject within it, we can omit **who** or **that**:

> Is everything OK with our order?
> – No, the documents *(that/which) you mailed to us last week* haven't arrived.
> Can I discuss the matter with someone else, please?
> – No, I'm afraid the person *who/that knows about this* is not available right now.

2 Non-identifying relative clauses give more information about a known person or thing. They are more common in writing than in speech. Notice the use of commas.

> Alex Brown, **who** *wrote to you about this*, is no longer with our firm.
> Getting a good job, **which** *everyone has a right to*, is not easy.
> The application form, **which** *is enclosed with this letter*, must be returned to us by April 24.
> Please telephone Ms Kurtz, **whose** *extension number is 666*.
> Mr Gray, **to whom** *you spoke yesterday*, is our Personnel Manager.

Notice that **whom** is more common in formal writing than in conversation:
We might write: but we'd say:

> The person **to whom** you spoke was ...   *The person you spoke to was ...*
> The people **with whom** I am working ...   *The people I'm working with ...*
> The man **from whom** I received the letter ...   *The man I got the letter from ...*

(B) Complete each sentence, using your own ideas. Add any commas that are necessary.

1 The qualifications that are mentioned in a job advertisement ..give.you.an.idea.whether..
..you.should.apply.for.the.job... – NO.COMMAS...

2 An interviewer who tries to frighten the candidate ....
....

3 On the other hand, an interview which is too relaxed and friendly ....
....

4 My friend Nick who feels very nervous at interviews ....
....

5 A handwritten letter which many companies prefer to a typed one ....

6 A CV which gives too much information ....

7 Your curriculum vitae which you should always send a copy of ....

8 Your application for the post which was mailed on 4 May ....

9 Unfortunately, the envelope in which your documents were sent ....

10 Mrs Mary O'Farrell with whom you have been corresponding ....

C Fill the gaps in these sentences with a suitable relative pronoun. Add any commas that are missing.

1 The person ...who... impressed me most was Mr Wright.   – **NO COMMAS**
2 Mr Wright .... application form we received yesterday is a very promising candidate.
3 His CV .... you showed me yesterday is most impressive.
4 He has excellent references from his present employers .... are ACME Engineering.
5 He was working in Norwich .... they have their HQ.
6 His qualifications .... you commented on are excellent.
7 The personnel officer .... interviewed him says that he's available at once.
8 The thing .... impressed her most is his personality.

D Make each of these pairs of sentences into a single sentence, using a relative pronoun.

1 She told us about her experiences in India. This was interesting.
   ...*She told us about her experiences in India, which was interesting.*...

2 I heard about the vacancy from a friend. This friend works in Personnel.
   ....

3 She gave me some information. This information was supposed to be confidential.
   ....

4 I heard about this from a colleague. This colleague assured me it was true.
   ....

5 Apparently, we sent the forms to an address. This address was wrong.
   ....

6 I had to fill in a six-page application form. This was very time-consuming.
   ....

7 I applied for a job. I saw this job advertised in the newspaper.
   ....

8 You gave a person's name as a reference. This person is unwilling to comment on you.
   ....

14 Sales and negotiation

14.1 Selling and negotiating   *Background information*

Selling

You don't have to be a special kind of person to sell a product. But although successful salespeople often have special talents and an outgoing personality, the skills they employ are used by us all: we build and maintain relationships with different kinds of people, we listen to and take note of what they tell us and don't just enjoy the sound of our own voices, and we explain things to them or discuss ideas with them.

A firm may depend on their own sales team and/or on the salesmanship of their distributors, wholesalers or retailers. But any company needs to establish a personal relationship with its major clients ('**key accounts**') and potential customers ('**prospects**'). It is often said that 'people do business with people': a firm doesn't just deal impersonally with another firm, but a person in the buying department receives personal visits from people representing the firm's suppliers on a regular basis – or in the case of department stores or chain stores, a team of buyers may travel around visiting suppliers.

Keeping salespeople 'on the road' is much more expensive than employing them to work in the office because much of their time is spent unproductively travelling. Telephone selling may use this time more productively (though in some countries this is illegal), but a face-to-face meeting and discussion is much more effective. Companies involved in the export trade often have a separate export sales force, whose travel and accommodation expenses may be very high. So servicing overseas customers may often be done by phone, fax or letter with not so many personal visits. Many firms appoint an overseas agent or distributor whose own sales force takes over responsibility for selling their products in another country.

A sales department consists of many people who are based in different parts of the country or the world, who don't have the day-to-day contact and opportunities for communicating with each other that office-based staff have. For this reason, firms hold regular sales conferences where their entire sales force can meet, receive information and ask questions about new products and receive training.

Negotiating

Diplomacy, friendliness and co-operation are important in selling. There's a widespread belief, which is probably true, that buyers 'buy from those they like' and that sellers give a better deal to 'those they like'. All salespeople have a certain 'fear', or reverence, for buyers because they have the power to give or to withhold an order. 'Negotiation' is the part of the sales conversation where bargaining about the conditions of an order takes place. It comes at the end of the sales talk at the point when the buyer is definitely interested. Because additional persuasion may be required, it's important not to give away concessions while making the sales presentation.

In international business there are different types of business negotiations, negotiation styles and negotiation situations. A simplified model of what goes on shows four main phases of negotiation:

1 The *preparation phase*: this is where you work out what you want and what your main priorities are.
2 The *debating phase*: this is where you try to find out what the other side or the customer wants. You say what you want but you don't say yet what the final conditions are. You use open questions and listen to

the customer to try to find out in what areas they may be prepared to move.

3 The *proposal phase*: this is the point at which you suggest some of the things you could trade or which you might theoretically be prepared to trade, offer or concede. Formulate your proposals in the form of *if ..., then ...* . Be patient and listen to the other side's proposals.

4 The *bargaining phase*: this is when you indicate what it is you will actually trade, offer or perhaps concede. In turn you conditionally exchange individual points, along the lines of: 'If you are prepared to pay swiftly, then we are prepared to change our delivery schedules.' Remember to write down the agreement.

Not all business negotiations take place face-to-face. Sometimes you may have to exercise negotiating skills on the telephone. Clearly, too, not all business bargaining ends in a deal. Some negotiations may begin with an exploratory session during which clients specify their needs and expect you to come back later with a proposal of how your company will meet those needs.

People often try to postpone a decision. They might politely break off from the negotiation and say something like: '*I'll have to think about it*' or '*I'll have to consult my boss or my department head*', etc. On the whole, however, people expect that agreement will be reached or else you'll do business with another company. Normally both parties are interested in reaching an agreement in which both sides take away something positive from the deal. This is called a '**win-win situation**'.

However, conflict can occur in business negotiations and relationships. Naturally, we all try to avoid this because this is where only one side can win and the other will lose. Situations which might lead to such negotiations could be late delivery, poor performance of a product, component failure or the need to make compensation payments. In a situation where one side is clearly in the wrong, the outcome is clear: either the conflict continues until the dispute is resolved or it goes to court.

The final important point about negotiating in the business world is the law of contract. It is generally enforceable in the courts. The position is more complicated in international business negotiations because of differences in laws and assumed liabilities. But, nevertheless, the courts are a source for remedies if contracts are broken. Suing defaulting contractors is quite common. A sound knowledge of contract law is therefore essential for negotiators drawing up an agreement at the end of a deal. However, this is the point at which the experts will usually have to be called in and so is not dealt with further here.

14.2 Of, out of ...   *Prepositional phrases – 4*

Fill the gaps in these sentences with a suitable noun and prepositional phrase. The first one is done for you as an example.

1 We are sending you our Spring catalogue ...**under separate cover.**...

2 Because the other items on the agenda were .... the meeting was adjourned.

3 It is at this stage of the process that any products .... are removed from the assembly line.

4 Even if the machines are ...., they should not be touched unless the power supply is off.

5 At a time when so many skilled workers are ...., it will be easy to fill the vacancy.

6 The old machinery was completely ....

7 .... your letter of 15 March, we are unable to offer you an alternative delivery date.

8 The strike was ...., so the production lost was minimal.

9 We'll have to reduce the workforce ...., perhaps by a process of voluntary redundancies.

10 We regret that we are unable to supply the items you ordered, as we are completely ....

of inferior quality   of minor importance   of short duration   out of date   out of order   out of stock   out of work   to a certain extent   under separate cover ✓   with reference to

A   ▢ᵏ◂ Study the following ways of giving advice. Highlight the ones you think are most useful.

If you want help or advice you use the following expressions:

> *What ought I to do?*
> *Do you think I should ...?*

> *I'd like your advice on ...*
> *What would you do if you were me?*

If you're talking to a person you don't
know very well you can say:

> *I would appreciate your advice on ...*
> *Could I ask for some advice on ...?*
> *I should like to ask ...*

If you don't want to sound too bossy you
can say:

> *Might it be an idea to ...?*
> *Have you ever thought of ...?*

Some more direct ways of making
suggestions or advising are:

> *If I were you I'd ...*
> *Why don't you ...?*
> *You'd better ...*

To advise a stranger or a business client, you
can say:

> *My advice would be to ...*
> *If I were in your position, I would ...*

> *I would recommend ...*
> *I would advise ...*

If you're going to accept the advice someone is giving you, you can say:

> *That's a good idea.*
> *That sounds great, I'll try it.*

> *Good idea, let's try that.*

But, if you don't wish to accept the advice, you can say:

> *No, I don't think I could do that.*
> *I'm not sure that's such a good idea.*

> *Well, perhaps another time.*

B   Decide which of the expressions below can be used for these functions:

a *asking for advice from a friend*
b *asking for advice from someone you don't know well*
c *giving advice indirectly*

d *giving advice in a direct fashion*
e *accepting advice*
f *rejecting advice*

Mark the expressions *a, b, c,* etc. The first one is done for you as an example.

1 That's a good idea ...   ...*e*..
2 If I were in your position, I would ...   .
3 Good idea, let's try that.   ......
4 I'm not sure that's such a good idea.   ......
5 I would appreciate your advice on ...   .

6 Could I ask for some advice on ...?   ......
7 Have you ever thought of ...?   ......
8 I'd like your advice on ...   .
9 Why don't you ...?   ......
10 Do you think I should ...?   ......

C ◎◎ You'll hear three short conversations. Answer these questions about each conversation.

1 How well do the people know each other?
2 What problem does each person have?
3 What advice does the other person give?
4 Does the other person accept the advice given?

Conversation 1

1 ....
2 ....
3 ....
4 ....

Conversation 2

1 ....
2 ....
3 ....
4 ....

Conversation 3

1 ....
2 ....
3 ....
4 ....

14.4 Talking shop   *Vocabulary*

Write the missing words in these sentences in the spaces in the puzzle.

1 We'll send you a .... of our product.
2 How can we .... sales without taking on more sales staff?
3 I've noticed that there has been a .... towards ordering later.
4 There is an enormous market for this product ....
5 ACME plc is our major ....
6 What .... of sales do you anticipate in your region?
7 We have built up a great deal of .... among our regular customers.
8 After that report on TV, we have had a lot of good ....

9 Even a company that has a .... invests in marketing and sales.

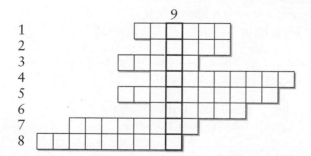

Read this article and then fill each gap below with one word.

CO-OPERATION AND COMPETITION IN NEGOTIATION

Negotiations are complex because one is dealing with both facts and people. It is clear that negotiators must above all have a good understanding of the subject. They must also be aware of the general policy of the company or institution in relation to the issues and they must be familiar with the organisational structure and the decision-making process.

However, awareness of these facts may not necessarily suffice to reach a successful outcome. Personal, human factors must be taken into account. The approach and strategy adopted in negotiating are influenced by attitude as well as by a cool, clear logical analysis of the facts and one's interests. The personal needs of the actors in negotiating must therefore be considered. These can include a need for friendship, goodwill, credibility, recognition of status and authority, a desire to be appreciated by one's own side and to be promoted and, finally, an occasional need to get home reasonably early on a Friday evening. It is a well-known fact that meetings scheduled on a Friday evening are shorter than those held at other times. Timing can pressure people into reaching a decision and personal factors can become part of the bargaining process.

Researchers who have studied the negotiating process recommend separating the people from the problem. An analysis of negotiating language shows that, for example, indirect and impersonal forms are used. This necessity to be hard on the facts and soft on the people can result in the sometimes complex, almost ritualistic, style of negotiating language.

Language varies according to the negotiating style. In negotiating you can use either a co-operative style or a competitive one. In the co-operative style the basic principle is that both parties can gain something from the negotiation without harming the interests of the other. Or in other words that both parties will benefit more in the long run in friendship and co-operation even if they make some concessions. This type of negotiation is likely to take place in-house between colleagues and departments, or between companies when there is a longstanding relationship and common goals are being pursued.

Unfortunately co-operative style negotiations without a trace of competition are rare. In most negotiating situations there is something to be gained or lost. There can be a danger in adopting a co-operative mode, as unscrupulous people may take advantage of co-operative people.

The opposite mode to co-operative negotiating is competitive negotiating. Negotiators see each other as opponents. Knowledge of the other party's needs is used to develop strategies to exploit weaknesses rather than to seek a solution satisfactory to both sides. This type of negotiating may be appropriate in the case of one-off contracts where the aim is to get the best result possible without considering future relationships or the risk of a breakdown in negotiations. Needless to say, the language in this type of discussion may become hostile and threatening even if it remains formal.

In reality most negotiations are a complex blend of co-operative and competitive mode. Negotiating successfully implies dealing appropriately with the four main components of any negotiation: facts, people, competition, co-operation.

Skilled negotiators are sensitive to the linguistic signals, as well as the non-verbal ones of facial expressions, gesture and behaviour, which show the type of negotiating mode they are in.

Language reflects tactics and therefore a study of the language used in negotiating brings a greater awareness of the negotiating process.

(adapted from *Negotiate in French and English* by Pamela Sheppard and Bénédicte Lapeyre)

1 Good negotiators must know their .... well and they must know their company's .... But they must also consider .... factors because they are dealing with ....
2 Negotiations are affected by the participant's ...., as well as logic.
3 Research has shown that it can help to separate the .... from the .... This can be done by using special negotiating ....
4 In a .... style of negotiation, the participants try not to harm each other's .... In order to maintain a good long-term .... they both make ....
5 In a .... style of negotiation the parties are .... This style may be suitable for a .... contract. The language here can become .... and ....
6 Most negotiations are a .... of the two styles. A good negotiator must be aware of the .... and .... signals which show the style being used.
7 The four main factors involved in a negotiation are ...., ..., ... and ....

You'll hear an interview with an experienced international business negotiator talking about different styles of negotiating in international business situations.

A ◎◎ Listen to the interview and decide which of these points is mentioned in the course of the talk.

1 English used in general international business situations ☐
2 the Americanization of the global economy ☐
3 the Japanese conversation style ☐
4 national characteristics as demonstrated in negotiating ☐
5 Europeans adopting the same style of negotiating ☐

B ◎◎ Listen to the interview again and match up what is said about the various nationalities' styles and what they do or what they are like in international negotiations, according to the expert.

Nationality	What they do / what they are like
Americans	are very well prepared
	make their points in a direct self-explanatory way
Brazilians	are direct – even blunt
	are distant
British	are extremely polite
	are indirect, even evasive
French	are informal and open
	are ordered and organized
Germans	are pragmatic and down to earth
	are thought of as pushy, even aggressive
Japanese	can appear direct and uncompromising
	choose their words very carefully
Spaniards	negotiate from a rational and clearly defined position
	hold negotiations up
Swedes	look people straight in the eyes
	make points in an indirect way

14.7 Order of adverbs   *Grammar review*

A Look at these examples, which show where you can place different adverbs and adverbial phrases in a sentence. The examples show the 'comfortable' places, though other, more emphatic, places can be used sometimes.

Adverb position

Before	Mid	After
Unexpectedly, the firm increased its profits.	The firm *unexpectedly* increased its profits.	The firm increased its profits *unexpectedly*.
Last year the firm increased its profits.		The firm increased its profits *last year*.
Recently the firm has increased its profits.	The firm has *recently* increased its profits.	The firm has increased its profits *recently*.
	The firm certainly *never* increased its profits.	

B Insert the adverbs on the right into the most 'comfortable' place in each sentence.

1 The corporate headquarters moved from Houston to Charlotte.	recently
2 The company realized that it was a profit-making area.	very quickly
3 Our sales staff worked the whole year.	hard
4 The machine was serviced by the engineer.	carefully
5 The production schedule will be achieved.	probably
6 The order book is stagnating.	currently
7 They check their inventory.	weekly
8 I'm sorry to say there is little we can do.	immediately
9 The customer delivered the cargo.	punctually
10 We have increased our product range in order to give our customers more choice.	gradually

C

Mid-position adverbs

Some adverbs often go in mid-position. Look at the examples and notice what is meant by 'mid-position'.

never   always   often   usually   once   rarely   hardly ever   frequently   ever obviously   probably   certainly   apparently   almost   nearly   completely just   hardly

We have *always* rewarded good work.   We *always* reward good work.
We can *always* reward good work.   Good work will *always* be rewarded.

D Insert the adverbs on the right into the correct position in each sentence.

1 There have been disputes with our suppliers.	rarely
2 Last year there were delays in concluding contracts.	frequently
3 The company went bankrupt as a result.	nearly
4 Now our firm is going to open a European factory.	probably
5 We would have accepted the offer.	certainly
6 Serious clients can expect to be told the facts.	hardly
7 You don't know what we're talking about.	obviously
8 The customers complain when we send John instead of Margaret to the sales conference.	always
9 Their operating expenses remained low.	apparently
10 The liaison officer forgot to inform the export manager's PA.	completely

E In these sentences the adverbs are in the wrong position. Move them into better positions in the sentences.

1 There has been a mistake definitely in this invoice.
2 European computer manufacturers are going apparently to work together on this project.
3 Do you think the firm ever will get the Chinese order?
4 The final price was much higher than occasionally the purchaser expected.
5 The customer was quite initially satisfied with our after-sales service.
6 We asked to see the chief negotiator before we made specifically the decision.
7 The CEO has announced just the export team for the Taiwan project.
8 We are going certainly to investigate the whole question as soon as possible.
9 If the correct procedure is followed you will have hardly ever a breakdown.
10 Although the freight carefully was handled, important components were broken in transit.

15 Revision

The exercises in this unit revise the skills and language points that you've covered in *New International Business English*. The exercises are not directly connected with the topic of Unit 15 in the Student's Book.

⚠ Your teacher may wish you to use some of these exercises as a progress test. In this case, please don't use the Answer Key while you're doing the exercises.

15.1 Grammar revision

Decide how best to fill the gap in each of these sentences, as in this example:

How many copies .... with the order?
a) did we sent
b) sent we
c) have we sended
d) did we send ✓

1 I remember asking him on the phone last November ....
  a) that the goods arrived on time.
  b) when the goods will arrive.
  c) if the goods would arrive on time.
  d) whether the goods arrived on time.

2 I can't find my glasses. .... them anywhere in the office this morning?
  a) Are you seeing
  b) Saw you
  c) Have you seen
  d) Did you have

3 Their product .... more imaginatively this season.
  a) is being marketed
  b) is marketing
  c) is been marketed
  d) is marketed

4 If we want to make a big impact, ... consider a TV campaign.
  a) we'll have to
  b) we better
  c) we had to
  d) we've got

5 A word processor is .... a typewriter.
   a) more easier to use than
   b) easier to use as
   c) as easy to use as
   d) not as easy to use than

6 If you .... ice in warm water, it soon melts.
   a) will place
   b) would place
   c) place
   d) placed

7 The level of discount .... the size of the order
   that is placed.
   a) is depending of
   b) depends of
   c) is depending on
   d) depends on

8 We are looking forward .... you at next
   year's conference.
   a) to see
   b) to seeing
   c) seeing
   d) that we will see

9 The warehouse entrance is .... the main
   car park.
   a) opposite to
   b) opposite of
   c) opposite from
   d) opposite

10 The new price lists .... tomorrow and will
   be available in a few days.
   a) are being printed
   b) are printed
   c) were printed
   d) will print

11 He told us that he .... for a new job.
   a) thought he would apply
   b) applied
   c) is applying
   d) had been applying

12 If the components .... delivered earlier we
   might have been able to start work on time.
   a) might have been
   b) were
   c) would have been
   d) had been

13 When .... writing the report of the meeting?
   a) have you finished
   b) are you finishing
   c) do you finish
   d) will you have finished

14 Mr Brown .... ten years.
   a) has been head of this department for
   b) is head of this department for
   c) is head of this department since
   d) has been head of this department since

15 The number of orders went up .... we increased
   our prices by 15%.
   a) because
   b) although
   c) when
   d) if

16 Mr Black is the .... office you'll be sharing
   this month.
   a) man, whose
   b) man, of whom the
   c) man of whom the
   d) man whose

17 These documents arrived on Thursday, ...
   a) arrived they?
   d) didn't there?
   c) didn't they?
   d) weren't they?

18 .... our new brochure, which should arrive next
   week.
   a) I just have sent
   b) I have just sent
   c) just I have sent
   d) I have sent just

19 When the post ...., I'll bring it into your office.
   a) will arrive
   b) arrives
   c) is arriving
   d) is going to arrive

20 .... an English course can be an interesting
   experience.
   a) To assist
   b) To attend
   c) Attending
   d) Assisting

15.2 Vocabulary revision

Here, for a change, is a complete crossword puzzle.

CLUES ACROSS

 1 Put down these arrangements to meet people in your diary (12)
 7 Payment in instalments (2)
 9 Money to start a business (7)
10 When several people run a firm and share the profits each is a .... (7)
11 Stamp dealers pay more for a stamp if it is .... (4)
12 Requests for goods (6)
15 How many millions are there in a billion? (8)
17 A project for the future (4)
20 Opposite of *hard* (4)
21 Employees receive these when they retire (8)
23 A customer gets one as proof of payment (7)
24 Against the law (7)
27 He or she deals with correspondence (9)
29 A self-employed business person has his or her .... business (3)
30 She always .... her name at the end of a letter (5)
31 These supply the raw material for paper (5)
32 Abbreviation for *Street* (2)

CLUES DOWN

 1 Open one at a bank (7)
 2 Money is printed on this (5)
 3 The extra you pay the bank for a loan (8)
 4 Another word for *until* (4)
 5 Opposite of *import* (6)
 6 A sales figure you aim to achieve (6)
 8 This department deals with recruitment and staffing (9)
13 This department deals with selling (5)
14 Money put into a business in the hope of making a profit (10)
16 Where business people spend most of their working hours (7)
18 A prediction of what something will cost (8)
19 'A .... and his money are soon parted' (4)
20 Stoppages of work due to industrial disputes (7)
22 An unusual business which employs clowns and animals (6)
25 A business supplies its clients with either .... or services (5)
26 Opposite of *borrow* (4)
28 When shareholders accept a take-over bid, they are saying '....' (3)

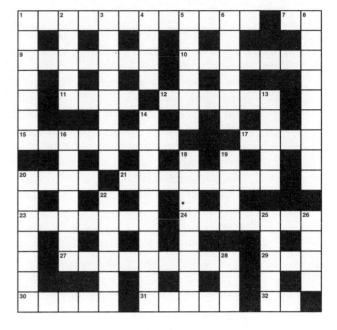

A Look at the expressions below. Which of them would you use to express each of these ideas?

What would you say …

1 if you do not want to accept the advice someone is giving you?
2 when you want to complain indirectly to someone?
3 when you want to tell someone a story?
4 if you haven't understood an explanation?
5 when you wish to agree with someone?
6 if you want to interrupt someone in a discussion to say something?
7 when it's unlikely that you can do something?
8 when you would like a person to do something for you?
9 when you want to give someone some information?
10 when someone you already know is introduced to you?

a) *Did I ever tell you about …?*
b) *Yes, I'm all in favour of that …*
c) *I doubt if we'll be able to …*
d) *I think you should know that …*
e) *I'm not sure that's such a good idea.*
f) *Yes, I think we've met before. Good to see you again.*
g) *There may have been a misunderstanding about …*
h) *Could I make a suggestion?*
i) *Do you think you could …?*
j) *I'm sorry, what did you say …?*

B Write down what you would say in these situations. Here is an example:

The receptionist tells you on the intercom that Mrs Martin has arrived.
...Oh good. Could you ask her to come up, please?...

1 Mrs Martin, a client, has arrived on her annual visit to your office.
....

2 She asks if she can make a long distance phone call after your meeting.
....

3 A plane flying over makes it impossible for you to hear the reason she gives.
....

4 She says her Christmas order didn't arrive till mid-January. You know this, but blame the shipping department.
....

5 She says that she called the shipping manager, but just got a rude, unhelpful reply. Thank her for this information.
....

6 Your new product will sell well – make sure she knows this.
....

7 She says your new product is just right for her market. You agree.
....

8 She asks you to show her how your new product works. How do you begin your explanation?
....

9 She wonders if she should place an order for 200 or 250 units.
....

10 You have just remembered an amusing experience. How do you begin telling Mrs Martin the story?
....

15.4 Word-building revision

Fill the gaps in these sentences with a compound word built from the word given on the right. Here is an example:

BP is a large ...*multinational*... corporation.   **nation**

1 Before operating the machine, you must .... the screws.   **tight**
2 You'll be impressed by the .... of this equipment.   **flexible**
3 The .... of their offices has cost a lot of money.   **modern**
4 The applicant is too .... for us to consider employing him.   **experience**
5 To say that exporting is profitable is an ....   **simple**
6 We've had complaints because the machine is ....   **rely**
7 We're still waiting for the .... of the loan we gave them.   **pay**
8 Turn the handle .... to open the door.   **clock**
9 She is a very good manager and ....   **administrate**
10 Thank you for your ...., it was very helpful.   **recommend**

15.5 Midway International   *Writing*

The situation

You work for Midway International, a trading company in your own country. One of your suppliers is Original Products plc in Scotland, who manufacture a range of high-tech products. One of your customers is Ultimate Pty in Australia.

Your company has received the letter below. Your boss, Mr Meyer, has told you to take appropriate action and he has left you some notes (see the Guiding points on the next page).

Original Products plc

20 Kirkton Campus   Livingston EH54 6QA   Scotland

```
Midway International
P.O. Box 777
K-4550 Euroville
Yourland                              April 2, 1999

Dear Mr Meyer,

Your order: MI/876

We regret to inform you that there will be a delay in
delivery of your order number MI/876 for 200 of our OP 232.
This is due to a number of problems we have been having
with the CPUs. We found that we were having to reject an
unacceptable proportion of these and it has been necessary
for us to look further afield for an alternative supply.
However, we have today secured the firm promise of a supply
of US-manufactured 68020s, which we expect to receive by
airfreight within the month.

As a result of using the 68020 instead of the original
68000, the processing speed of the unit is now slightly
reduced from 12.0 MHz to 9.7 MHz. This should present no
compatibility problems for users.
```

May I take this opportunity of asking you for some feedback on
our OP 424 series products? We are keen to
have information on your own and your customers' reactions
to the price, packaging and design of these units. Also,
if you have any comments on the performance and reliability
of these units, perhaps you could let me know as we have
been getting some unconfirmed reports of failures.

Thank you very much for your help and patience.

Let me assure you that we will make our best efforts to
expedite your order.

Yours sincerely,

Janet McArthur

J. McArthur (Mrs)

Telephone: 44 1506 444777   Fax 44 1506 33881

Write two letters or faxes:
Ⓐ to Original Products plc, Ⓑ to Ultimate Pty.

You are on first-name terms with Bruce Dundee of Ultimate, but not with Mrs
McArthur of Original Products.

Guiding points (Make sure you deal with all these points.)

Ⓐ Guiding points for letter or fax to Mrs McArthur:

> 1 *Hurry up or we will cancel order – we must receive the units by 1 May*
> 2 *Make sure we have priority over other customers*
> 3 *Speed of the unit is considerably slower than specification – our customers may not find this acceptable and price should be $45 lower*
> 4 *re feedback on OP 424 series: we'll ask our own customers for comments*
> 5 *We have one OP 424 in our head office: seems to overheat, but hasn't broken down – yet!*
> 6 *In case of breakdown, should users return defective units to your factory?*

Ⓑ Guiding points for letter or fax to Mr Bruce Dundee, Ultimate Pty, 4130 Pacific Drive,
Brisbane, Australia:

> 1 *Apologize for delay in supplying order UP/901 for 10 OP 232s*
> 2 *Explain reasons for delay*
> 3 *We plan to ship to you on 2 May by airfreight – or earlier if possible*
> 4 *Mention our worries about speed reduction – will this affect you?*
> 5 *Manufacturer may reduce price – we'll pass this saving on to you*
> 6 *Ask for feedback on OP 424 series*
> 7 *Ask if any OP 424s have broken down*
> 8 *Send greetings to Sheila (Bruce's wife)*

Read the text carefully, then choose the correct answers to the questions below.

PEARL RELOCATES

The Pearl Group is to relocate its London headquarters and five regional offices to Peterborough in a move involving 2,000 jobs.

Pearl has obtained a 20-acre site at Peterborough Business Park, on which it will develop a 250,000 square feet building at a cost of £25 million.

Construction is planned to start next spring, with the new building ready for occupation two years later. In the meantime, Pearl will start moving staff into temporary accommodation in Peterborough later this year.

It is the second major endorsement of Peterborough by the Pearl Group.

Some years ago, Pearl Assurance obtained a 10-acre' site from the Peterborough Development Corporation at Thorpe Wood for its computer and accounts centre.

The 400 staff who currently work at Thorpe Wood will transfer to the new offices and the older building, says Pearl, "will be surplus to requirements and will be further developed as an investment."

A further 1,600 staff employed by the Group will be given the opportunity to move to Peterborough. Pearl estimates that its relocation decision will create an annual demand of between 200 and 300 jobs in the Peterborough area.

Group Chairman Einion Holland said: "To maintain its position as one of the UK's leading life offices, Pearl must be able to offer its customers the products they want at the right price.

"This requires the combination of operational flexibility and efficiency and low costs, which it would have been impossible to achieve at our existing Chief Office.

"The ability to centralise our operations in Peterborough and to develop the most up-to-date computer systems which only a purpose-designed building will allow, will bring important long-term benefits for our customers, shareholders and employees."

Pearl has occupied the same High Holborn building since 1915. Now the entire building is in need of major refurbishment, but no decision has yet been made about its development.

It is estimated that among the long-term savings created by the move to Peterborough will be running costs of £1 million a year, and London weighting of £2 million.

Peterborough beat off competition from other places because of Pearl's experience of the successful earlier relocation, and because of the quality of the site at the business park.

For Peterborough, it is the biggest single relocation out of more than 420 firms attracted since the city's expansion programme began, beating the move of travel organisation Thomas Cook from London to Thorpe Wood which involved more than 1,000 jobs.

Development Corporation General Manager Kenneth Hutton said: "This is the best news we have had. We have been working on this project for many months, and we knew that Pearl was looking at several other places very seriously. Peterborough won because it was the best."

THE PETERBOROUGH EFFECT

1 Before they acquired the 20-acre site, Pearl Group …
   a) already had one site in Peterborough.
   b) already had two sites in Peterborough.
   c) had no sites in Peterborough.

2 Staff will start moving to Peterborough …
   a) shortly before the new building is completed.
   b) when the new building is completed.
   c) long before the new building is completed.

3 When the new building is complete, Pearl's Thorpe Wood building will …
   a) be used as temporary offices.
   b) not be used by Pearl.
   c) be used as its computer centre.

4 The new building in Peterborough Business Park will house Pearl's …
   a) headquarters.
   b) headquarters and five regional offices.
   c) headquarters, computer and accounts centre, and five regional offices.

5 Pearl plan to relocate to Peterborough so that …
   a) they can redevelop their London head office.
   b) they can operate efficiently and keep costs low.
   c) their products will be more competitive.

6 Moving to Peterborough will save Pearl …
a) £1 million a year.
b) £2 million a year.
c) £3 million a year.

7 Peterborough was chosen, rather than another location, because of …
a) Pearl's successful relocation of its computer and accounts centre.
b) Peterborough's closeness to London.
c) Thomas Cook's successful relocation to Peterborough.

8 When Pearl's new building is complete …
a) 1,600 employees will have to move to Peterborough.
b) 400 employees will move to Peterborough.
c) 1,600 employees can move to Peterborough if they wish.

9 After the move, the total number of Pearl employees in Peterborough will be …
a) 200 to 300.   b) 1,600.   c) 2,000.

10 Pearl Group's business is …
a) manufacturing.   b) life assurance.   c) travel services.

15.7 The Peterborough Effect – 2   *Reading*

Read the text, then choose the correct answers to the questions on the next page.

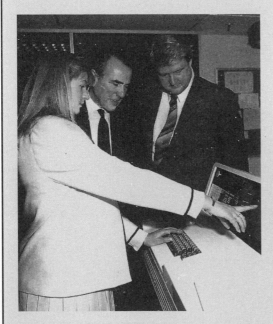

Americans choose city as a pivot for European trade

An American firm which uses the most sophisticated communication equipment has chosen Peterborough as the pivot between its European customers and manufacturing plants around the world.

Chesterton (UK) Ltd is part of Chesterton International, a specialist engineering group based in Massachusetts.

Its new European Customer Service Centre has been set up in offices in a converted older building on the edge of Peterborough's Queensgate covered shopping centre.

The new centre will receive orders from all parts of Europe, translate them, and pass them to the Chesterton factories in Holland, Eire and the USA.

Each of its Peterborough staff has mastery of at least one European language – and all but one of them were recruited from the locality.

Chesterton specialises in pumps and sealing devices used in the process industries. International Manager Philip Metz said: "Peterborough was chosen because it was the place which best met our criteria of central location, high technology communications capability and the availability of highly educated quality staff."

The Peterborough operation is a return "home" for the company, which was formed 102 years ago by A. W. Chesterton soon after emigrating from the East Midlands town of Loughborough.

THE PETERBOROUGH EFFECT

1 Chesterton's Peterborough offices are ...
   a) purpose-built.
   b) near the shopping centre.
   c) extremely attractive.

2 The new centre will receive orders ...
   a) from European countries.
   b) from all over the world.
   c) from the United States.

3 The new centre is being set up because ...
   a) it is expensive for customers to communicate with the USA direct.
   b) orders are placed in many different languages.
   c) Chesterton has so many factories in Europe.

4 Every member of the new centre's staff can speak English and ...
   a) one or more European language.
   b) more than one European language.
   c) one European language.

5 The new centre's staff ...
   a) all come from Peterborough.
   b) mostly come from the Peterborough area.
   c) all come from the Peterborough area.

6 Chesterton's business is ...
   a) communications.
   b) processing.
   c) manufacturing.

7 Peterborough was chosen because of its location and because ...
   a) the founder of the company came from the East Midlands.
   b) Chesterton has no factories in the UK.
   c) suitable staff were available.

15.8 Prepositions revision

Fill the gaps in this text with the right prepositions, as in this example:

   We must give priority ...*to*... export orders.

1 There is a lack .... information .... that company.
2 We still have 200 boxes .... order .... you.
3 The consignment consists .... four large crates .... all.
4 Max was left .... charge .... the department for too long.
5 He signed the documents .... behalf .... his company.
6 She retired .... the firm .... the age of sixty.
7 .... reference .... your order, we apologize for the delay.
8 We always insist .... payment .... advance.
9 Can you deal .... this report in time .... the meeting?
10 I've never visited Britain .... business, only .... holiday.

You'll hear a recording of part of a training session for small business people on the principles and practice of franchising.

A Before you listen to the recording, read this introductory text:

FRANCHISING

The principle of franchising is that the **FRANCHISOR** sells an established, successful business format to a **FRANCHISEE**, who will carry on the business in a clearly defined territory.

All franchises trade under the same name and appear to be branches of one large firm, not independent companies. In the USA, most of the well-known fast food restaurant chains and hotel/motel chains are actually franchises. Some examples are: McDonald's restaurants, Budget Rent-A-Car and Tandy/Radio Shack stores.

B Listen to the first part of the recording. Fill the gaps in this summary.

The franchisor usually supplies:

1 an .... product or service and a well-known .... image.
2 an .... manual, showing how the business should be set up and how it must be run.
3 help, advice and training in .... the business.
4 continuing advice, training and support during the .... of the franchise.
5 the .... that's required to set up and operate the business.
6 .... of the product, which he will be able to .... cheaply in .... This may result in savings or, depending on the franchisor's mark-up, ... the franchisee to buying at .... the market price.
7 local, national and even international ....

C Listen to the second part of the recording and answer these questions about it:

1 The questioner points out that ...
  a) franchisees usually require varying amounts of on-going support.
  b) franchisors tend to reduce their on-going support a year after start-up.
  c) not all franchisors give the same quality of support.

2 She also points out that, as a franchisee, you must find out ...
  a) what brand image and support the franchisor is providing.
  b) what level of help you will be getting after a year or so.
  c) what level of help you will get when you start up the franchise.

3 In the case of problems in running the franchise, you need to know:
  a) Will the franchisor be able to solve all your problems?
  b) Will the franchisor provide financial support in an emergency?
  c) Will you be offered regular advice by the franchisor?

4 In his answer, the lecturer points out that the franchisee should find out what help he/she will get from the franchisor ...
  a) in recruiting staff.
  b) in training his/her present staff in new skills.
  c) in training new staff.

5 You should also find out whether ...
  a) the franchisor will continue to research and develop the product.
  b) the product has been thoroughly researched and developed.
  c) the franchisor will charge you a levy for R & D.

6 You need to know whether the franchisor is ...
  a) continuing to advertise the product.
  b) spending as much on advertising as the franchisees are charged.
  c) spending enough money on advertising.

7 The lecturer goes on to say that a franchisee pays the franchisor ...
  a) a substantial capital sum.
  b) a monthly fee.
  c) both a capital sum and a monthly fee.

8 To raise money to pay for a franchise, a franchisee ...
  a) will probably have a lot of difficulty in getting a bank loan.
  b) will probably have little difficulty in getting a bank loan.
  c) must have an enormous amount of money in the bank.

9 The franchisor's income from a franchise is calculated on the basis of ...
  a) the franchisee's net profits.
  b) the franchisee's total sales.
  c) the franchisee's net monthly income from the franchise.

10 If a franchisee wants to sell the franchise to someone else ...
  a) he/she must have the franchisor's permission.
  b) he/she must pay the franchisor a substantial commission.
  c) he/she is not allowed to do this, he/she must sell it back to the franchisor.

Finally ...

Dear Reader,

Congratulations on finishing the exercises in the Workbook! We hope you've enjoyed using New International Business English as much as we've enjoyed writing it!

Goodbye and best wishes,

Leo Jones   Richard Alexander

Answer Key and Transcripts

1 Face to face

1.2 Around the world
Vocabulary

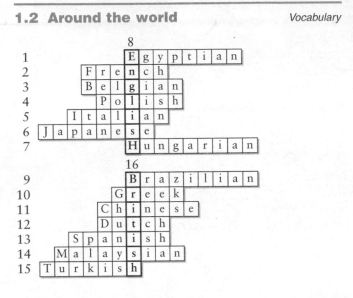

1.3 Go along and get along
Reading

True: 2 3 5 6   False: 1 4

1.4 Have you met ...?
Functions & speaking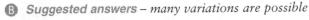

B *Suggested answers – many variations are possible*

2 Hello, Tony. Nice to meet you.
3 That's right, yes, we once worked together in ...
4 I'm terribly sorry, I've forgotten your name.
5 Yes, good morning, my name's ___. I've got an appointment with ...
6 Did you have a good journey? It's very nice of you to come all this way.
7 Would you like a coffee? *or* Would you like something to drink?
8 Good heavens, is that the time? I didn't realize it was so late. I really must be going now.

1.5 Asking questions
Grammar review

A *Suggested answers – many variations are possible*

2 Did you have a good flight?
3 Who would you like to see?
4 Who did you speak to last time you came?
5 Who recommended this particular hotel to you?
6 Are you travelling alone?

7 How long are you planning to stay?
8 Has your husband been here before?

B *Suggested answers – some variations are possible*

3 How long have you been working here?
4 Which room do you keep your sales files in?
5 Why do you never phone in the morning?
6 When did you start working for the firm?
7 What kind of room would you like?
8 Who did you hear about this product from?
9 How much does the complete package cost?
10 How many copies of the report did they print?
11 What did they ask you to do?
12 Who told you that you should get in touch with us/me?

C

3 ..., won't they?
4 ..., can't we?
5 ..., can they?
6 ..., is she?
7 ..., does it?

8 ..., don't you?
9 ..., haven't you?
10 ..., should we?
11 ..., mustn't we?
12 ..., has he?

1.6 Do it my way
Reading

True: 3 4 5 7 10   False: 1 2 6 8 9

2 Letters, faxes and memos

2.2 It's in the mail
Vocabulary

2.3 Joining sentences

Grammar review

B

2 I often choose to write although a phone call is quicker.
3 I usually telephone in order to save time.
4 Please check my in-tray while I am away at the conference.
5 I shall be able to confirm this after I have checked our stock position.
6 I shall be able to confirm this when I have consulted our works manager.
7 We cannot confirm the order until we have checked our stock position.
8 Please reply at once so that we can order the supplies we need.
9 Please reply as soon as possible because we do not have sufficient stocks.

C

2 The package was so heavy that a single person couldn't lift it.
3 Although the order arrived late, we were able to supply the goods on time.
4 In spite of fog at the airport, our plane landed safely.
5 Because of a mistake in the hotel booking, I had to find another hotel.
6 In order to give them the information at once, I sent them a fax.
7 Due to an error in the shipping department, their order will have to be checked again.
8 While we've been talking, my assistant has handed me the file.

D *Suggested answers – some variations are possible*

2 Because your letter to us and our letter to you were both posted yesterday, the letters crossed in the post.
3 Our company has a long tradition but our letters look old-fashioned and, as we are trying to modernize the company's image, all our correspondence should be word-processed.
4 Because short sentences are both easy to write and understand and long words can be confusing, a simple style of writing letters is recommended.
5 Although a letter should have a personal touch and people like to be treated as individuals, it is unwise to use a style that is too informal with people you don't know very well.

E *Model answers*

I am sending you our latest catalogue, as you requested, and I feel sure that it contains plenty to interest you. Can I draw your attention to our new range of colours? These will brighten up your office and help to keep your staff feeling happy.

If you work in an export department you need a lot of specialist knowledge. This includes mastering the complex documentation and being aware of the various methods of payment that are available. You also have to be able to correspond with foreign customers.

Writing to people you haven't met face-to-face is difficult. The hardest part is establishing a personal relationship with them, so that you can show them that you are a real person, not just a machine that writes letters.

2.4 Can you tell me how to spell that?

Speaking

The correct spellings are given in the recording:

In the odd-numbered sentences, the second spelling is correct.
In the even-numbered sentences, the first spelling is correct.

Make sure you can spell the words out loud easily and fluently, and not just write them correctly.

2.5 Correcting spelling and punctuation mistakes

Writing

A These are the 13 spelling mistakes:

Madam enclosed which received information quite further products catalogue *or* catalog available discount pieces compatible

B The punctuation mistakes have been corrected here:

I am afraid that we have not been able to contact you by telephone. My secretary called throughout the day yesterday at half-hourly intervals but was told that you were "not available". Please contact me personally as soon as possible because we need to check a number of details in your order.

You can reach me by telephone at any time this afternoon or tomorrow morning. Our office hours are 8.30 to 5. You can leave a message for me to call you back if necessary.

➡ The title above has been corrected!

2.6 Abbreviations

Vocabulary

1 Street Square
2 12th July 7th December
3 number
4 care of attention
5 for example that is and so on (et cetera)
6 public limited company Limited and Company
7 Corporation Incorporated
8 postage and packing value added tax
9 carbon copy enclosed/enclosures postscript
10 at 3,000 yen each copyright registered trade mark trade mark 'What you see is what you get'

2.7 Make a good impression

Writing

This improved version of Mr Burke's letter shows just one way the letter could be written – many variations are possible.

Dear Mr Brown,

Thank you very much for your order.

Unfortunately, in common with other suppliers, our prices have risen since you placed an order with us two years ago, but you will be pleased to hear that we will supply your current order at the old price.

I enclose our new catalogue and price lists, which contain several exciting new products and our latest prices.

I will keep you fully informed about the progress of your order. If you would like to get in touch with me urgently, our new fax number is 998321 or, of course, you may prefer to phone me.

Yours sincerely,
A. Burke
Sales Director

3 On the phone

3.2 Telephone techniques
Listening

1 position
2 right person
3 brief
4 bad line   call back
5 Smile
6 technical   abbreviations
7 names   quantities
8 interrupt
9 lunch hour
10 Note down

Transcript

Training officer: Right. I think the best thing is if I give you some rules. If you make notes now, you can ask questions and we can discuss what I've said afterwards. Is that OK? . . . All right.

Right, first off: give your name slowly and clearly. Identify yourself and your position in the company, all right? Just make sure you're talking to the correct person. Right, after that, say right away what you're calling about, don't expect the other person to guess this or work it out. Plenty of mistakes are made that way! Be brief, remember that the other person may have other things to do than to talk to you on the phone.

Right, also if it's a bad line, say that you'll call back at once. Then ring back and start the call again. OK? Speak slowly and clearly, but in a friendly voice and *smile*! All right? The other person can hear if you smile. Don't let the other person misunderstand your attitude as being, you know, unfriendly.

Ah, right, don't use technical terms or abbreviations, because the other person may not understand these as well as you do. Also give important information, like figures, names, quantities, dates and so on, slowly and carefully. Repeat all the important information. Make sure that the other person has noted it down correctly – especially numbers, which are often the most difficult thing to understand over the phone. Also let the other person finish speaking – don't interrupt him or her even if you think you know what he wants to say. That's...they'll take it as very rude.

Ah...if possible, don't phone during the other person's lunch hour or just before they're about to stop work for the day, right? Find out what time it is in the other country before you call. I mean, think about it from your own point of view, I mean if you're heading off for a sandwich you don't want to have to be on the phone for an hour or so before . . .

Also note down all the important information you're given by the other person. OK? You don't want to have to waste the phone bill calling up again.

Now, if you do all this, you can prevent misunderstandings occurring. OK, well, if you have any questions, anybody?

3.3 Using the phone
Vocabulary

1 dialing/dialling   ringing   busy/engaged
2 area code
3 collect call/transferred charge call
4 person-to-person call/personal call
5 off the hook

3.5 Speaking and writing
Functions

Suggested answers – *many variations are possible*

2 Would you mind confirming this by fax?
3 I regret to say that we are unable to offer you a special discount.
4 Please let us know if you would like us to send you a sample of this product.
5 With your permission, we propose to ship the order in two separate consignments.
6 Thank you very much for your kind assistance.
7 If you have any questions about our literature, do please let me know.
8 Unfortunately, we are unable to make amendments to an order by telephone.

3.6 Who's speaking?
Vocabulary

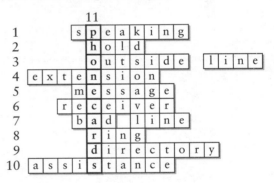

3.7 Three messages
Listening & note-taking

The missing information is in bold type:

1 SUSAN GRANT of Richmond Studios called about order for 1 x MQ 20, sent 3 weeks ago – on **5th** of this month.
Sent you cheque for **£425** to get it at special offer price but no **acknowledgement** of order.
Please confirm receipt of order and **special price**.
Any problems, phone Susan Grant on 0303 **518136**.
When can she expect **delivery**?
Address: **14** High Street, Woodbridge, **Ipswich**, IP12 4SJ

2 PETER **REDFORD** of Eastern Enterprises in **Boston** called:
Can't **make it to meeting** on **Friday** afternoon because of problem with hotel – no room because of **fire**.
All other hotels in town full because of **convention**.
Will come on Monday morning (**23rd**) if OK with you.
Please tell him if this change of date is **not OK**.
Please call him if you have ideas for **solving accommodation problem** on 617 **032 0876**.

Answer Key and Transcripts

3 **ALEX BROWN** called:
Staying 2 extra days in **Los Angeles** and trying to get flight back on **14th**. Direct flight is full – they've put him on **the waiting list**.
May not be back till **Wednesday 17th**.
If not back, please take over at meeting on Tuesday with **Orion International**.
All info in file on his desk with **Olivia Flaubert**'s name on.
Please collect O.F. from **Talbot** Hotel first thing in the morning.
Any problem: leave a message at his hotel (**213 666 4529**) or send fax (**213 875 4114**).

Transcript

1 This is Susan Grant. I'm calling about my order for one MQ 20, which I sent you by post about three weeks ago on behalf of my company, Richmond Studios. I sent Mr Collins a cheque for £425 with my order, so that I could get it at the special offer price you advertised till the end of the month. The problem is that I haven't received any acknowledgement of the order. Could you please confirm that you have received my order and that you can ship me the goods at the special price. If there's likely to be any delay or any other problem, could you please phone me, Susan Grant, 0303 518136. The order was sent on the 5th of this month. I'd like to know when I can expect delivery, please. The company address is 14 High Street, Woodbridge, Ipswich (IPSWICH), IP12 4SJ. Thanks very much.

2 Hello, this is Peter Redford, calling from Eastern Enterprises in Boston. I've got a meeting with Mr Collins on Friday afternoon. I'd like you to tell him that I'll be unable to make it, I'm afraid. The reason is that there's a problem with the hotel accommodation I booked over the telephone: they've had a fire and now they can't let me have a room. I've tried other hotels in the town, but they're all full because of the convention. The only thing I can do is to come up to see Mr Collins on Monday morning, that's the 23rd, if that's OK. I'll assume this change of date is OK if I don't hear from you. Oh, if Mr Collins has any good ideas for solving the accommodation problem, please call me at this number: 617 032 0876. OK? My name again is Peter Redford – that's REDFORD. OK. Thank you very much. Goodbye.

3 This is Alex Brown. I'd like…I'd like you to give Mr Collins a message when he gets back. Here's the message: I've got to stay an extra two days here in Los Angeles and I'm trying to get a flight back on the 14th. The problem is that the direct flight is full, so they've put me on the waiting list. This means I may not be back in the office till Wednesday, that's the 17th. If this is the case, I'd like Mr Collins to be ready to take over if I can't make it to the meeting on Tuesday with Orion International (that's ORION). All the information he requires is in the file which is on my desk. It's the one with Olivia Flaubert's name on (that's OLIVIA FLAUBERT). He'll need to pick her up from her hotel first thing in the morning, she'll be staying at the Talbot Hotel (that's TALBOT). If there's any problem you can leave a message for me at my hotel (on um…213 666 4529) or send a fax to the hotel for my attention (on 213 875 4114).

3.8 Call me back
Vocabulary

A	B
1 pick up	1 lift
2 call back	2 return the call
3 look up	3 find
4 put through	4 connect with
5 cut off	5 disconnected
6 get through	6 reach
7 hold on	7 wait
8 give up	8 stop trying
9 hang up	9 replace the receiver
10 is over	10 has finished

3.9 Present tenses
Grammar review

2 picks up	7 prints out
3 deserve	8 get through
4 's/is assisting	9 'm/am putting you through
5 's/is looking up	10 'm/am making
6 'm/am attending	

2 … how do you usually keep in touch with him?
3 … which shipment is being unpacked now?
4 … What does the specification look like?
5 … where is she working at present?

Ⓓ

2 … in fact we aren't making it up this week.
3 … actually it doesn't print out the figures every day.
4 … in actual fact I'm not working as Mrs Green's assistant.
5 … actually they don't always deliver the goods promptly.

4 Summaries, notes, reports

4.2 Punctuation

To: Departmental Manager
From: Human Resources Manager
Date: 15 September

Subject: Overseas Trainee Placement Scheme

As requested, I enclose a copy of the scheduled programme for the Trainee Initiation Week. It will be held from 23 October to 27 October.

Following your secretary's telephone call, I have set aside a session for you to speak to the participants. I have scheduled this for Monday 23 October, starting at 3.00 pm.

I am now completing the final arrangements for the week. Accordingly, I would be grateful if you could confirm that the proposed time on Monday will be convenient for you.

In addition, I would also appreciate receiving any comments you may have on the programme by Friday of this week, if possible.

4.3 Summarizing

 Listening & speaking

A

In the first conversation the woman feels disappointed because it wasn't her fault she didn't get the job.

In the second conversation the people are in a happy mood because the sales contract has been signed.

Transcript

Conversation 1

Woman: Well, I came in the front door of this great big office building and there was this huge plant or a tree. I…I don't know what it was. It was just being delivered off a very large lorry. I could hardly get through the main door. So, the doorman and receptionist were extremely busy. It took about ten minutes before I finally found out where the interview was and where it was supposed to be taking place and all that. So, I went in the lift. You know it was one of those gigantic modern steel-plated affairs. I…I pressed the button for the fourteenth floor. There was another girl in there and a man with a toolbox or something. Anyway, the lift stopped and the man got out and do you know what happened? The lift started to move and then stopped between the eleventh and twelfth floors. Fortunately the girl in the lift with me said they'd been having a lot of trouble with the lift and there was no need to panic. She pressed one of the buttons and spoke to this man called Joe and explained the lift had got stuck. She was incredibly cool. Anyway, after what seemed ages to me, it must have been about, oh, ten minutes, the lift slowly moved up to the twelfth floor. And when the door opened, there was a man standing there. It was the man who'd just got out of the lift. By that time, of course, I was extremely late for the interview. So I ran up the stairs after I'd found them. And that took some time. Well, as you can imagine, things didn't get off to a good start. I explained everything, but in the end I didn't get the job. They said they wanted someone with a lot of experience with using data processing systems. But I still believe it was because I'd got there so late. You know, first impressions and all that…

Summary of Conversation 1

The woman was late getting to the job interview. She thinks this is the reason why she didn't get the job.

Conversation 2

First woman: Well done, John! Terrific news. If anyone was going to do it was going to be you.

Second woman: Yes, we all said it, you know. There was no one else in the department who could have managed it in such record time.

First woman: Yes, when did you first visit them?

Man: Oh, about the beginning of March, I think it was.

Second woman: Really? And it's only, well, what's the date today? The fifth.

First woman: That's right.

Second woman: Gosh, it's only the 5th of July, now. Goodness me, I must congratulate you, once again. I never thought we'd be sitting around so soon and celebrating.

First woman: John, you really are a genius!

Man: Well, it's not just me. I mean the whole local sales force have to take some of the credit.

Second woman: But you got them to sign on the bottom line, and that's the important thing.

Summary of Conversation 2

The two women are congratulating the man on signing a sales contract with a client in a very short period of time.

B

Summary of Conversation 3

Samantha's colleague seems to think she's planning to leave her job.

Summary of Conversation 4

The two colleagues are discussing whether they can make the delivery to Tarrasco or not, or whether IBO will have to wait. They decide to deliver to Tarrasco first. The spare drivers will be able to make the delivery.

Transcript

Conversation 3

Man: What's the matter with Samantha these days?

Woman: Why do you ask?

Man: Well, she wasn't at the meeting about the pay rise.

Woman: That's right. Do you think she's getting restless?

Man: Well, she did tell me about her fiancé wanting to move away from town.

Woman: But so what? That might not last.

Man: True, but I saw her studying the jobs vacant page last week in a coffee break.

Conversation 4

Man: Look, we can get the Tarrasco stuff out next Thursday. Send them a telex.

Woman: But we just sent one, telling them the shipment would be sent out today.

Man: Yeah, yeah, I know, but the situation has changed now, hasn't it?

Woman: Perhaps.

Man: What do you mean, perhaps?

Woman: Maybe we can still get Tarrasco's stuff out tomorrow, if the lorry is back from the Asado run.

Man: Yes, but the drivers need some rest. I mean, you know, they'll have been out delivering for three days non-stop. You can't send them out again tomorrow. No. Send out a telex, as I said. I mean it would have been all right, but we've got to service IBO first. Their order has preference, you know.

Woman: But I think IBO can wait, too, surely. They said they were holding up production for a week.

Man: I know, but their order is all packed up and ready to go.

Woman: But the Asado drivers can still rest and we'll send out the spare team. No problem.

Man: Ah, do you think so?

Woman: Yes, sure. Look, they'll be glad of the overtime and travel bonus. And we'll have the order there on time, just the same. And the day after tomorrow, we'll send the other team out again.

Man: OK.

Woman: They can do the IBO run, and a few other things I've got lined up in my in-tray here.

4.4 Getting it down on paper

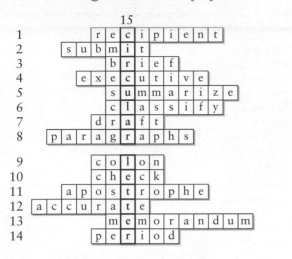

```
                    15
1          r e c i p i e n t
2        s u b m i t
3            b r i e f
4        e x e c u t i v e
5              s u m m a r i z e
6              c l a s s i f y
7            d r a f t
8      p a r a g r a p h s

9              c o l o n
10             c h e c k
11         a p o s t r o p h e
12   a c c u r a t e
13             m e m o r a n d u m
14           p e r i o d
```

4.5 Dealing with a report

The correct order of the paragraphs:
3   7   5   1   8   4   2   6

True: 1   3   5   7
False: 2   4   6   8   9   10

4.6 Rule Number One: Clear that desk

1 not   clear   2 year   3 45   4 untidy
5 40   6 minute   hour   7 Act   Pass   File   Throw

4.7 The passive

Hopefully, you noticed that the *wh-* questions require answers with the passive and the *yes/no* questions those with the active. The passive emphasizes more *what* is affected, while the active lays the stress on *the person* who is involved in the action.

1 b   2 a   3 f   4 e   5 d   6 c

2 Payment is enclosed together with our order.
3 The delivery should be received by Friday.
4 He may have been notified before the invoice arrived.
5 FCS's new dental equipment is only being marketed in Europe.
6 The premises have been enlarged since my last visit.
7 Similar investments are being made in other parts of the world according to a recent report.
8 The notes were finally found under the filing cabinet.
9 The components will be produced at our São Paulo factory.
10 Costs would be reduced if less paper were used.

2 The suppliers will make further modifications to this service to other customers.
3 Ordinary office staff can easily operate the systems.
4 You can master the new software easily in a couple of days.
5 Using better trained staff has achieved increased productivity.
6 The department now sends out invoices a week earlier.
7 You can only achieve better results if you work harder.
8 We shall introduce the new note-taking method in our office.
9 I should warn you about the dangers of not co-operating with the personnel manager.
10 The organizers will supply all relevant information about the meeting in advance.

5 Working together

5.2 Firms at work

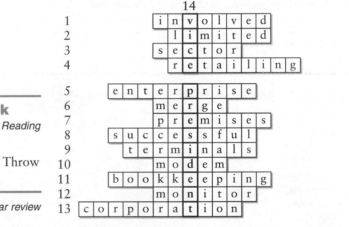

```
                    14
1            i n v o l v e d
2              l i m i t e d
3          s e c t o r
4            r e t a i l i n g

5        e n t e r p r i s e
6              m e r g e
7              p r e m i s e s
8        s u c c e s s f u l
9            t e r m i n a l s
10             m o d e m
11       b o o k k e e p i n g
12           m o n i t o r
13   c o r p o r a t i o n
```

5.3 Prefixes

1 re-   2 pre-   3 sub-   4 multi-   5 out-   6 over-   7 mis-
8 trans-

1 outlook
2 outlived   replacing
3 preprinted
4 miscalculated
5 overcharged
6 redesign
7 multinational
8 sub-contracted
9 sub-let
10 prefabricated

5.4 Agreeing and disagreeing

Functions & listening ◎◎

Conversation 1

TOPIC: Smoking should be forbidden in offices.

1st woman	✓
1st man	✓
2nd woman	✗
2nd man	✗
3rd man	✓
3rd woman	✓

Transcript

1st woman: I think it's time that smoking was forbidden once and for all in all offices.

1st man: I agree entirely. And I think the management should be firm on this. It should be abolished on the firm's premises.

2nd woman: Now wait a minute. I can't say I share your views on that. The staff should be asked to vote first.

2nd man: Now, that's just what I was thinking. We don't live in a dictatorship, you know. I think grown people should be allowed to decide for themselves if they want to smoke or not.

3rd man: Maybe, but don't you think non-smokers' health can suffer if the smokers are allowed to continue?

3rd woman: Quite right, I couldn't agree more. And it might also be a way of educating people to live and work in a more healthy fashion.

Conversation 2

TOPIC: All companies should offer their employees free lunches.

1st man	✓
1st woman	✓
2nd man	✗
2nd woman	✓
3rd man	✓
4th man	✓
3rd woman	✗

Transcript

1st man: You know what, I think all companies should offer their employees free lunches.

1st woman: Quite right, I couldn't agree more with that. After all if we have to work here all day and have no time to go home in the lunch hour it's only fair.

2nd man: I can see what you mean. But what happens if the canteen food doesn't suit you? Or just isn't tasty?

2nd woman: That's a good point. But I still think free lunches are a good idea. The company should have to give the employee the money to buy their own, if the lunches are not satisfactory.

3rd man: Yeah, I'm all in favour of that. The company made very high profits last year. They can afford it.

4th man: I couldn't agree more. They could offer a wide variety of dishes to suit all tastes. It would be only fair.

3rd woman: Hm, I see things rather differently myself. I would like my lunch hour left to myself to decide where and what I eat.

Conversation 3

TOPIC: Overtime should be abolished so that people without jobs can find work.

1st man	✓
1st woman	✓
2nd man	✗
2nd woman	✗
3rd man	✗
4th man	✓
3rd woman	✓

Transcript

1st man: It's quite clear that overtime should be abolished so that people without jobs can find work.

1st woman: Yes, I'm all in favour of that. It would mean that lots of extra jobs could be created.

2nd man: Well, my opinion, for what it's worth, is that the employers are not prepared to take on additional staff. They say it would be too expensive.

2nd woman: Now, that's just what I was thinking. And another thing. If overtime is cut, it'll simply mean that we'll have to work twice as hard in normal working hours for the same money.

3rd man: I don't think it's a good idea either. The people who are unemployed are not necessarily the ones who have the skills to do our jobs.

4th man: Perhaps, but don't you think we need to demonstrate to the management that we are prepared to consider alternatives to increased overtime. Anyway, my wife and family are sick of not seeing me as much as they could.

3rd woman: That's a good point and we should also emphasize that the company should take on unemployed people and retrain them in the necessary skills they might not possess.

Conversation 4

TOPIC: Managers should have far more control over what employees do.

1st man	✓
1st woman	✓
2nd man	✗
2nd woman	✗
3rd woman	✓
3rd man	✗

Transcript

1st man: You know, I believe that we managers should have far more control over what employees do.

1st woman: You know, that's exactly what I think. We need to know what work they are doing at every point during the day. That is the only rational way to organize an office today.

2nd man: I can't say I share your views on that. My employees are not machines. They're human beings. In my experience you get work done far more efficiently if you allow employees to work at their own pace.

2nd woman: Now, that's just what I was thinking. The important thing is to allow each individual to work at a certain number of tasks, but not to watch over them too closely. They do a better job that way.

3rd woman: I can see what you mean, but my experience shows that only certain employees can be left entirely alone. The rest need watching closely or else they waste the firm's time. And they are here to work after all.

Answer Key and Transcripts

3rd man: Maybe, but don't you think, there is a limit to how closely we should watch our staff? After all, I don't know about you, but I only have one pair of eyes. I can't watch 25 people all at once and do my own work at the same time.

5.5 Prepositions – 1

2 based on
3 approved of
4 advertise for
5 account for
6 apply to
7 benefit from
8 blamed   for
9 backlog of
10 bid   for

5.6 The eternal coffee break   *Reading*

1 comfortable chat/talk   2 not   3 meet/gather
4 heart/centre   5 time busy   6 do where   7 social
8 departments not

5.7 Referring to the past   *Grammar review*

 B

2 hasn't stopped
3 opened
4 started
5 has been looking
6 were having
7 sent   haven't received
8 used to work   moved

C

1 RENATE was born in Karlsruhe, Germany in 1964.
2 She studied Economics and Computing at the University of Munich from 1984 to 1990.
3 In 1991 she joined Biofoods as a computer operator.
4 Since 1993 she has been a trainee manager.
5 She has been responsible for Southern Europe since February 1995.

6 PIERRE was born in Amiens, France in 1950.
7 From 1971 to 1977 he studied electrical engineering at the University of Nantes.
8 After this he worked for General Electronics in San Diego, USA from 1978 to 1985.
9 In 1985 he joined Biofoods.
10 He has been head of Export Sales in Basle since 1989.

6 International trade

6.2 Documentation   *Vocabulary*

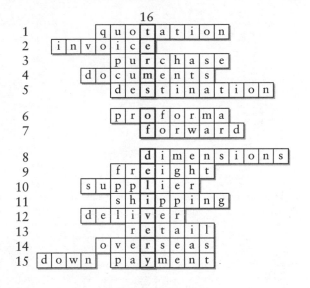

16

1 quotation
2 invoice
3 purchase
4 documents
5 destination
6 proforma
7 forward
8 dimensions
9 freight
10 supplier
11 shipping
12 deliver
13 retail
14 overseas
15 down payment

6.3 Making enquiries   *Speaking & writing*

A

1 4   5 010 852 5667890
2 13 January   6 300 x 400 x 300 mm
3 7 or 8 February   7 5.85 kg
4 Johnson Brothers

B *Model fax*

To Mr Chan, Orion Electronics

Re: Our order number 355

Dear Mr Chan,

We have a number of questions about this order:

1 How many separate consignments will there be?
2 What date will the first consignment be shipped?
3 What is the expected date of its arrival here?
4 What is the name and phone number of your freight forwarders?
5 What are the dimensions and weight of each package?

Please note that our Mr Field is in Hong Kong next week. He will call you to arrange a meeting.

Looking forward to hearing from you.
Best wishes,

6.4 Sales and delivery   *Vocabulary*

1 volume   margin
2 cash with order   cash on delivery
3 bill of lading   bill of exchange
4 retail   point of sale   value added tax   wholesale
5 inventory/stock   backlog   hold-up
6 special delivery   crates
7 grade   premium   bulky   surcharge
8 tender   triplicate   deadline

6.5 What do they want to know? *Reading*

1 c 2 c 3 a 4 c 5 b (the error is in the latter, i.e. the last one mentioned)

6.6 'J.I.T.' *Listening*

 B

The points that were mentioned: 1 2 4 7 9 12

C

Missing words: 2,000 200 orders co-operation / cooperation design quality plant stock economic

Transcript

Interviewer: One of the phrases that we're hearing more and more in business these days is 'Just in Time' – it's an idea that seems to be overturning traditional ideas of industrial production. Carl Feldman is research adviser to the Industrial Association. Carl, what exactly is 'Just in Time'?

Carl Feldman: Well, the underlying philosophy of 'J.I.T.', as we now call it, is that of eliminating waste. Manufacturing, ideally, should work on a day-to-day basis. Depending on the type of industry this might be stretched up to a week-by-week basis, but not any longer. A manufacturer should only manufacture a product that he has an order for and should only carry a stock of materials for what he will make on a single day. Now, most companies carry stock for several days, even for several weeks – fearing that if they…if they run short of a particular material, their entire production process will be disrupted.

Interviewer: Yes, but surely this is true? If just one component is lacking, then production does have to stop.

Carl Feldman: Yes, but the point is that it's a waste of money, having capital tied up in materials that won't be used for several days. And you save money if your materials arrive just in time to be used in the manufacturing process.

Interviewer: Where does J.I.T. originate from?

Carl Feldman: The story is that a group of Toyota engineers from Japan were touring industrial plants in the USA, on the lookout for new methods of improving efficiency – this was in the 1970s. They were impressed by what happened in the supermarkets they went into: they noticed that as soon as a shelf in a supermarket was nearly empty, a shelf-filler came along and topped it up. They simply applied this principle to manufacturing. So that's how it all started.

Interviewer: Now, an accountant would insist that you have to keep your workforce busy all the time and keep your machines running at all times. This maximizes your efficiency.

Carl Feldman: With J.I.T. you only run machines if you have a product to make. In most manufacturing, the cost of materials is around 60% of the total costs of running the business, so any materials sitting unused in a warehouse can't begin to repay their costs until they have been turned into a product. The traditional accountant's view has to be reassessed.

Interviewer: But in any industry there are fluctuations in demand. How does J.I.T. cope with this?

Carl Feldman: In the same way that capital tied up in materials is being wasted, making products for stock also ties up capital. If there are no orders for a particular day, there is no logic in making for stock. Both machines and workforce have to be grouped by product, not by function, so that they're flexible enough to deal with fluctuations – which may mean more work on some days and less on others.

Interviewer: So how do you keep the workforce busy on a slack day?

Carl Feldman: There's time then for maintenance, training and so on – particularly important these days is quality.

Interviewer: So, to come back to the supply of materials, this depends on the co-operation of your suppliers, then?

Carl Feldman: Absolutely! And changes in philosophy are essential here too. Most major companies obtain materials from over 2,000 different suppliers, with J.I.T. this number has to be cut down to around 200. The benefit to the supplier is that he will get more orders from you if he can work with you in this way. Inevitably, this involves very close co-operation on the design and quality of the materials he supplies and he must adopt the J.I.T. philosophy in his own plant. If not, he'll find that the pressure is on him to hold stock for his customers – and this will clearly not be economic.

If a supplier can't cope with J.I.T., then he'll find that major companies will simply find other suppliers who can.

6.7 Prepositions – 2

2 compensate you for
3 cope with
4 comment on
5 credit your account with
6 comply with
7 co-operate with
8 collaborating with
9 cut back on
10 capable of
11 consists of
12 convince them of

6.8 Looking into the future *Grammar review*

B *Suggested answers*

2 What time does the train from Birmingham arrive?
3 Where are you meeting Ms Carpenter before the conference?
4 If I call you before 5 pm, will you still be in your office?
5 Will you let me know when the goods arrive in your warehouse?
6 When will you have finished typing the report?
7 What will you be doing after the meeting this afternoon?
8 When are you going to write/send a fax to ACME Industries …?

C

2 Tomorrow, I'm going to ask the boss for a rise and that's definite!
3 By the time I retire, I'll have been working *or* I'll have worked here for 10,000 working days.
4 She's flying to Spain on Tuesday to meet our clients in Seville.
5 I'll put the documents in the post to you first thing tomorrow.
6 Please don't disturb me for the next half hour, I'm going to phone Tokyo.
7 Excuse me, Mr Grey, when are you going to write *or* will you be writing to our Chinese clients?
8 While you are in Stockholm, will you be seeing Mr Olsson?
9 Stand back, everyone, he looks as if he's going to sneeze!
10 Don't worry, I'm sure the spare parts will arrive soon.

D

1 When will you be able to ship the goods to us?
2 When does the plane from Bombay land here?
3 What is she going to apply for?
4 How long will you be staying here?
5 When are you leaving work this afternoon?

E

2 Oh no, they aren't going to be rejected – they're going to be accepted!
3 Oh no, he won't still be working on it – he'll have finished it!
4 Oh no, I don't start work late – I start work quite early!
5 Oh no, it isn't going to run reliably – it's going to break down!

7 Money matters

7.2 Financial terms
Vocabulary

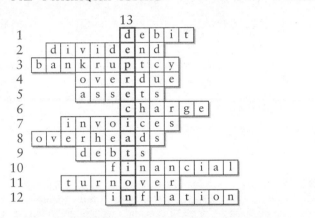

7.3 Numbers and figures
Speaking & listening ◎◎

B

The missing figures are underlined.

Profit before tax at £210.4m was ahead by 10.6% on turnover of £2,126.1m, up by 4.6%. We must allow for the 1995 review of chemists' labour and overhead costs, as well as the net impact of currency fluctuations. Adjusting for these, profits were ahead by 12.8% on turnover up by 7.3%.

Retail Division turnover at £1,832m increased by 4.2%, and profits at £130.7m were up by 11.1%. UK sales and profits increased by 5.5% and 10.6% respectively, before property disposal surpluses.

Industrial Division achieved sales of £404.9m, an increase of 5.7%, with profits of £66.6m, ahead by 3.7%. At comparative exchange rates these increases become 11% and 15.6% respectively. The UK retail sales increased by 5.5% from an unchanged sales area.

7.4 The Co-operative Bank
Reading

1 survive   2 invest   3 support   4 1870s 1992
5 bad/harmful   6 beliefs/policy/values   7 speculate
8 other where

7.5 Suffixes – 1
Word-building

B

2 stylish
3 affordable
4 financial
5 quarterly
6 vocational
7 cautionary
8 optional
9 statistical
10 systematic

7.6 Prepositions – 3

2 involved in
3 interfere with
4 have a look at
5 dispose of
6 give priority to
7 equivalent to
8 have confidence in
9 dealing with
10 insure against

7.7 Taking a message – numbers
Listening ◎◎

1	Qty	Description	Unit Cost
	26	Model 4 Phasers Type 4/7A	$14.25

2 Invoice No. **1450468**

Job Reference **287456398**

Marks & Numbers
HAWB 13576

Qty	Description	Unit Cost
250	Artemis Type 66A plus batteries	$58.75

3 Invoice No. **GR 375**

Job Reference **91/754**

Marks & Numbers
1 package

Qty	Description	Unit Cost
100 sheets	Type 4479 44 x 72 cm heavy paper	$22.35

4 Invoice No. **98645**

Job Reference **365776**

Marks & Numbers
3 packages

Qty	Description	Unit Cost
475	Type D89 switches	DM 5

Transcript

1 Can we just go through that once more, please? That was invoice number 5968. And the job reference is 177205039. And it was 26 Model 4 Phasers, type 4/7A. At a unit cost of 14 dollars and 25 cents. Good, I think I've got all that. Goodbye till next time. Thank you.

2 I'd just like to check that again. That's 250 Artemis Type 66A plus batteries. At a unit cost of 58 dollars 75 cents. And it was invoice number 1450468. And the job reference is 287456398. And, most important, of course, under the marks and number of packages heading: H-A-W-B 13576. Good, I think that's all then. Goodbye till next time. Thank you.

3 I'd just like to check that once more, please. That's 100 sheets of type 4479 44 by 72 centimetre heavy paper. At a unit cost of 22 dollars and 35 cents. And it's invoice number GR 375. And the job reference is 91/754. Then under the marks and number of packages heading: 1 package. Good, I think that's all then. Goodbye till next time. Thank you.

4 Can we just go through that once more, please? This is invoice number 98645. And the job reference is 365776. Let's see, that was 475 Type D 89 switches. At 5 deutschmarks each. And, under the marks and number of packages heading: 3 packages. That's it then. Right, thanks a lot.

7.8 Reported speech
Grammar review

B *Suggested answers* The underlined forms have been transformed or added.

2 She <u>wondered whether</u> it could have been delayed.
3 He <u>said that he didn't</u> know. <u>He had</u> no delivery note.
4 She <u>said</u> that the problem <u>was</u> that <u>they had</u> no record of payment.
5 He asked her whether <u>that was</u> the reason why <u>she was</u> ringing <u>that day</u>.
6 She <u>emphasized</u> that <u>his</u> firm <u>had</u> always <u>been</u> such regular payers in the past.
7 He <u>said that they had</u> a cash-flow problem at the moment.
8 She <u>asked</u> what <u>he proposed they</u> do.
9 He <u>asked whether she could</u> let <u>them</u> have just ten days.
10 She <u>agreed</u>. But she <u>said that it / that would</u> be the absolute limit.

8 Dealing with problems

8.2 Delays and problems
Vocabulary

1 merchandise   reject   refund
2 transit   compensate   claim
3 truck/lorry   load   rebate
4 minor   major   modification
5 expired   void
6 circumstances   storage
7 boycotts   quotas
8 cash against documents   documents against payment
  Chamber of Commerce

8.3 Take it back, son
Reading

True: 1 5 8
False: 2 3 4 6 7

8.4 Take a message
Listening & note-taking

A The missing words are in bold type.

Call from **Henri** Morand, **Transocéan** S.A., Bordeaux.
Both AR 707s running for 6 weeks now. Did usual routine tests before installing them in labs but now one unit is **noisy**.
Makes a loud harsh **vibrating** noise, as if drive motor is **unbalanced** or one of the heads touching **side of case**. Happens **2 or 3** times a day.
After **30 secs** noise stopped and **readings** normal.
Question: Is this a fault they should **worry about**?
If it is a problem that needs fixing they can **send the unit back**.
Please confirm that this will be **at our expense** and they can have **replacement unit** immediately.
Or they have unit examined by local **expert** – at our expense.
Call him **at home** tomorrow am on **56 52 60 44**.

B *Model fax to Mr Morand*

To Henri Morand
From (your name)

I am sorry to hear of your problems with one of your AR 707 units. I don't think you need worry about the vibrating noise. But to set your mind at rest we have instructed our agent to visit you next week to examine the unit. Our agent, Ace Importers, will be in touch with you on Monday.

Best wishes,

C

Call from **Byron Santini**, **Sunrise** Electronics, Toledo, Ohio.
Re: upgrade of 4 x **Sunrise 3** Drives with new hardware options.
He understood we would ship them at **our expense**, then they would upgrade for **$250** per unit, then ship them back to us at **their expense**.
This arrangement was **confirmed** in our fax to them of **July 7**.
Problems: 1 They've only received **1 drive**.
          2 We've **charged** their agents here for air freight and **insurance**.
Proposal: They will upgrade drive number **R 9290004** and **charge** us for air freight and insurance. Please **confirm this is acceptable**.
Question: Were other 3 drives sent at the same time?
If so, maybe **lost in transit**.
If not, **send them right away but** at our expense.
Call him tomorrow **before 6 pm** their time (**419 897 4567**) or send fax (**419 897 0982**).

N.B. If they don't hear from us, they'll **hold the one drive** they've received and **withdraw the special price of $250** for the upgrade!

D *Model fax to Mr Santini*

Dear Mr Santini,

Thank you for your telephone message. I apologize for the misunderstanding about shipping costs. Please inform your agents that there will be no charge for air freight and insurance.
   We accept your proposal to upgrade drive number R 9290004 and charge us for air freight and insurance.
   The remaining three drives have not yet been packed and

shipped. As soon as we have received back the first drive and it is running again, we will send them to you at our expense.

Thank you for your patience.
Sincerely,

Ⓐ Transcript

Mr Morand: This is Henri Morand (HENRI MORAND) from Transocéan S.A. (TRANSOCEAN) in Bordeaux. You sent us two of your AR 707s by air freight, which arrived safely last month. We've had both units running for six weeks now. Now, we did the usual routine tests on them before installing them in our laboratories but now that we have them both in use, we've found that one of them seems to be rather noisier than the other. Every so often one of the units seems to make a very loud sort of harsh vibrating noise, as if the drive motor is unbalanced or one of the heads is touching the side of the case. This happens for no apparent reason two or three times a day, and it always happens with the same unit. The first time it happened we were terrified because we thought the whole unit was about to blow up! But after about half a minute the noise stopped and the readings were normal. Now we don't really want to take the unit out of service, as the performance of the unit seems to be unaffected and we can't really do without it now.

So what we'd like to know is this: is this a fault that we should worry about or not? If it is a problem that needs fixing (and I assume you would know this from your after-sales reports on other units) we can send the unit back to you, but if we do I'd like you to confirm that this will be at your expense and that we can have a replacement unit immediately. The alternative is for us to have the unit examined by a local expert – again at your expense.

So can you let us know which of these alternatives you recommend? If you can call me at home tomorrow morning, please, I'd be very grateful. The number is 56 (that's the area code) 52 60 44. All right?

Ⓒ Transcript

Mr Santini: This is Byron Santini (BYRON SANTINI) calling from Sunrise Electronics of Toledo, Ohio. As you know, we arranged to upgrade four of your Sunrise 3 Drives to incorporate the new hardware options and my understanding was that you would ship these to us at your expense and that we would then carry out the upgrades here for the nominal charge of $250 per unit and ship them back to you at our own expense. You confirmed this arrangement in your fax to us of July 7. Now the problem is that we've received only one of the drives and, according to the documentation, our agents in your country have been charged for the air freight and insurance!

What we propose is that we carry out the upgrade on this drive (its serial number is R 9290004) and we'll charge you for air freight and insurance from us to you. Can you confirm that this is acceptable?

I'd also like to know: did you send the other three drives at the same time? If so, they may have got lost in transit if they haven't arrived yet. If you haven't, then please send them right away but at your expense, in accordance with our original agreement.

Can you call me in my office tomorrow before 6 pm our time (the number is 419 897 4567) or send us a fax (the number is 419 897 0982) to let us know how you wish to proceed? If you don't get in touch, we will hold the one drive we have received until we hear from you and we will withdraw our special price of $250 for the upgrade. So the ball's in your court, my friend. OK?

8.5 After-sales
Vocabulary

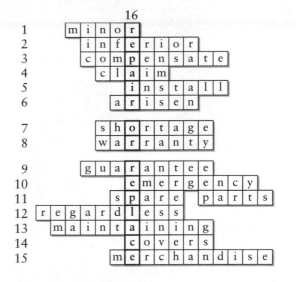

8.6 Apologies
Functions

Suggested answers

3 I'm terribly sorry I didn't call you back yesterday.
4 I'm awfully sorry, Mr Brown. I'm afraid I misunderstood your instructions and mailed the wrong documents to our supplier.
5 Excuse me, Mr Brown, but you know those sales figures you gave me? Well, I seem to have mislaid them.
6 I'm very sorry about this, but I'm afraid we put the wrong date on the invoice we sent you, so we're sending you a new one.
7 That's quite all right. I've only been waiting about a quarter of an hour.
8 You remember that instruction manual I asked you to send us? Well, it still hasn't arrived. Could you send it quickly, please?
9 Excuse me, Mr Brown, you said you'd call our clients in Dallas. Is there still time this afternoon?
10 Oh, I'm very sorry to hear that, Ms King. I'll check it myself personally and call you back before lunch.

8.7 Bean sticks to its back yard
Reading

1 mail order 2 quality 3 many 4 others Bean
5 return replacement refund 6 satisfying
7 sorry/unhappy

8.8 Prepositions – 4

2 negotiating with
3 make a large profit on
4 put pressure on
5 placed an order for with
6 lack of
7 proportion of

8 I object to
9 merged with
10 notify us of
11 looking forward to
12 order larger quantities from

8.9 What if ...?

Grammar review

2 breaks down   we'll (will/shall) call *or* contact
3 is   will be carried out
4 had made   would have accepted
5 would   do   saw
6 realized   would know   *or* knew   would realize
7 refuse   we'll (will/shall) send
8 had foreseen   would have checked

© Suggested questions

2 How would you feel if you were promoted?
3 What would you do if you were going to America to work?
4 Where would you go if you won a lot of money?
5 What would you do if you owned your own company?
6 What would you do if tomorrow was a day off?
7 What will you do if it's raining tomorrow?
8 What would you have done if your car had broken down yesterday?

©

2 But if they hadn't installed a new computer, things wouldn't have got worse.
3 But if the software had been tested, the system wouldn't have broken down.
4 But if orders hadn't been delayed, customers wouldn't have complained.
5 But if the phone lines hadn't been overloaded, customers would have been able to get through.
6 But if there hadn't been a lot of/so many problems, customers wouldn't have looked for a more reliable supplier.
7 But if their products hadn't been excellent, many customers wouldn't have remained loyal.
8 But if the software hadn't been improved, they wouldn't have started to catch up on the backlog.

©

2 in case
3 unless
4 when
5 if *or* when
6 until
7 in case
8 until *or* unless

9 Visitors and travellers

9.1 Going abroad   *Vocabulary*

9.2 Air travel in the USA

Reading & listening ◉◉

® Suggested answers

2 fly to Orange County (John Wayne Airport) or Hollywood-Burbank Airport
3 wait for your plane
4 won't be any cheaper
5 avoid a busy gateway like New York, Miami or Los Angeles – Charlotte, Pittsburgh and Orlando are less busy

© Suggested answers

1 be delayed because too many flights are scheduled to take off around that time.
2 get anything to drink or eat.
3 frightened, especially if you're in the clouds.
4 you get a guaranteed seat and a free phone call to the person who is meeting you the other end.
5 airports will be especially busy.
6 O'Hare (Chicago), Atlanta or Denver.
7 check it in – take it as hand baggage.
8 something to eat and drink in your hand luggage.

Transcript

Presenter: Nigel Isaacs is editor of *Business Travel Weekly*. Nigel, what kind of problems do airline passengers face in the USA?
Nigel: Most of the problems are caused by the heavy volume of traffic. All airports have a limit to the number of takeoffs and landings they can handle.
   All flights from a hub arrive and leave at more or less the same time: if 60 aircraft are scheduled to take off between 5 pm and 5.15 and the airport can only handle 120 an hour that means some will always be late landing or taking off. And if the weather is bad . . . So, passengers have to be loaded into each plane and then the planes have to line up to take off.

Crossword answers:
1 visa
2 economy
3 hire
4 transfer
5 postponed
6 route
7 bill
8 set meal
9 dessert
10 conference
11 translator
12 interpreter
13 delegates
14 check in
15 convention
16 visitor

There's a marvellous story of the people who'd been waiting for over an hour for their plane to reach the head of the line to take off, when they heard the captain on the intercom telling them that he was so fed up he was quitting his job, and he walked through the cabin, opened the door, jumped to the ground and walked off across the tarmac!

Queueing on the tarmac is frustrating (with no drinks or meals available until you're in the air), but queueing in the air with other planes circling just below you and above you is downright terrifying. Especially if you're in the clouds.

Another problem that's very common is overbooking: you hear an announcement on the airport loudspeakers: 'We have oversold on this flight and would like volunteers to go on the next flight out.' If you decide to volunteer, you may get a cash bribe, or a free trip voucher – but make sure you get a guaranteed seat on the next flight and a free phone call to whoever is meeting you the other end. Worse still you arrive with a confirmed reservation and you discover you've been bumped off the flight. There's another story of a man who was raising hell when this happened to him and he said to the check-in clerk, 'If I was a Senator, you'd get me a seat' and the man behind him in the line said, 'Son, I am a Senator and they won't give me a seat either.'

Presenter: Presumably, if you choose to travel at off-peak times, there are no problems.

Nigel: Well, there are no off-peak times – all flights seem to be full, except Saturday, oddly enough. If there's a public holiday, things are likely to be especially busy: Thanksgiving in November, Labor Day in September, Independence Day in July and so on. The special fare systems on the airlines' computers encourage more people to fly on less popular flights and this means that as a result all flights are equally full.

Presenter: So what advice would you give to a traveller in the USA?

Nigel: The worst hubs are O'Hare (Chicago) and Atlanta and Denver because they have so many flights – I'd say these are to be avoided at all costs.

Don't ever check your baggage if you can help it.

And be prepared for delays – take something to eat and drink in your hand luggage.

9.3 Travelling
Functions

Suggested answers

2 I'd like to change my reservation on flight LJ 879 on May 16 to flight ZZ 857 on May 17.
3 Is it too early to check in for flight RA 372?
4 Excuse me, could you show me how to get a ticket from this machine?
5 The main railway station? Yes, you go down this road for two blocks and then turn left. You can't miss it.
6 I'm terribly sorry I'm so late. I rented a car and it wouldn't start, you see.
7 Could you explain some of these dishes on the menu for me, please?
8 I'd like to have just a plain omelette, if that's all right.
9 Can you recommend a nice local dish?
10 Oh, do let me pay for this, please.

9.4 Negative prefixes
Word-building

un-	*dis-*	*in-*	*non-*
undesirable	disconnect	incapable	non-payment
unemployed	dishonest	inconvenient	non-profit-making
unforeseen	dissatisfied	inexperienced	non-stop
unfortunately		informal	
unknown		insufficient	
unreadable		invalid	
unused			

anti-union	semi-official
semi-circle	semi-permanent
anti-government	semi-automatic
semi-professional	

2 non-stop
3 insufficient
4 illegal
5 dissatisfied
6 invisible
7 anti-clockwise/counter-clockwise
8 invalid
9 Unfortunately
10 unforeseen

9.5 Prepositions – 5

2 retired from
3 resigned from
4 report on
5 running short of
6 regardless of
7 qualified for
8 range from ... to
9 reduction in
10 responsible for
11 ran out of
12 report to

9.6 What the clever traveller knows
Listening

B Suggested answers

2 in your hand luggage.
3 an RTW (round the world) ticket.
4 a ticket to Buenos Aires and not using the Rio to Buenos Aires leg.
5 Bahrain, Hong Kong and Taipeh.
6 staying away for more than two weeks.
7 allow time for delays and breakdowns.
8 get to know a good travel agent.
9 finding out which airlines offer a free seat for your spouse.
10 becoming eligible for 'special customer status'.

Presenter: Here's Nigel Isaacs again with some more advice for business travellers. Nigel, welcome back. So what kind of mistakes do inexperienced travellers make?

Nigel: The first mistake business travellers make is to take far too much luggage. You don't need ten clean shirts – your hotel can wash and press them for you. So take only carry-on luggage: at most airports you can get away with two small bags. If you do have to check in any baggage, make sure all your important documents are in your hand luggage – you know the old joke: breakfast in London, lunch in New York, luggage in Nairobi.

Another mistake people make is to think that you have to pay full price for air tickets. You should find out about the different ticket options: for example, an RTW fare can save up to 40% on normal fare.

Presenter: RTW?

Nigel: Round the world. For example, if you're going to Australia, you could go out via Singapore and come back via North America. Another way to save money is to see if a ticket to a destination beyond is cheaper. For example, a ticket from London to Buenos Aires via Rio may be cheaper than London to Rio, so you can book through to Buenos Aires and don't use the next leg of the flight. Or Amsterdam–London–New York may be cheaper than London–New York.

But don't be tempted to go for the cheapest possible fare: going to Japan via Bahrain, Hong Kong and Taipeh may be cheaper than flying non-stop but it takes quite a long time to recover!

Another mistake is to go away for too long. Most people's efficiency and energy starts to fall off after two weeks away. So, keep your trips short: only go for two weeks – and never for longer than three.

Don't expect everything to go according to plan. Expect the unexpected: there may be heavy snow in July or your taxi may break down on the way to the airport. In other words, don't be optimistic about plans. Don't schedule important meetings too closely together – allow time for delays and breakdowns.

And another thing: get to know a good travel agent and make sure he gives you the best possible service. Take discounts for example. A good travel agent can get first class for the price of business class and he does enough volume of business to get discounts with airlines on his own behalf, which he should pass on to you – so make sure he does.

Another thing worth knowing is that some airlines have lower fares if you travel at less popular times of day and some offer a free seat for your husband or wife. It's worth finding out about these – again it's your travel agent whose job it is to know about these things. A travel agent who deals with a lot of business travel is obviously going to know more about these things than one whose main trade is package tours to Spain.

Presenter: How about accommodation?

Nigel: Not everyone realizes that almost all hotels offer discounts. Your travel agent, if his turnover is high enough, should be able to offer up to 50% off certain hotels in other parts of the world. If you regularly stay in the same hotel, you should be eligible for 'special customer status' – that means you get rooms at a discount or frills like double for the price of a single or late checkout – if you're lucky you can get both discount and frills.

Presenter: I think the worst parts of a trip are having to travel overnight or get up at 3 am to catch an early flight. Or being stuck for a weekend in some dreadful industrial city. Are there any ways of avoiding that?

Nigel: Yes, a weekend break or a stopover in a more relaxing or lively city is often available at a special cheap weekend rate – various airlines and hotel chains offer these and it's always more pleasant to stay the night in a hotel than on a plane, even if you are in business class. For example, for no extra charge you can spend an evening somewhere nice like Copenhagen, Madrid or Vienna before a long-haul flight the next morning.

9.7 *To be* or not *to be* ... or *be -ing* ?

Grammar review

Ⓐ *Suggested answers*

1 Visiting / Arriving in   Staying / Living / Spending nights
Getting/Driving
2 going to / visiting / flying to
making / making sure you have / confirming
phoning/calling
3 going/travelling   waiting / sitting / having to wait
trying/tasting/sampling
4 to stay / to spend a night   to spend
to get / to book / to obtain
5 eating/sitting / to eat / to sit
to catch / to take / catching / taking
to chat /to talk / chatting / talking
6 making/taking   to answer / to pick up
to send   meeting / seeing / being introduced to
to reach / to get / to contact / to get in touch with
calling/phoning
7 to meet / to see   to discover / to find out / to read
to get / to come   to meet / to wait for
8 heavy/expensive/bulky
to get / to find / to be sure of getting

Ⓑ

2 to find out
3 to post
4 to avoid   going
5 to buy
6 having
7 to get
8 to get

Ⓒ

2 to get / to have   to visit
3 to spend
4 to find
5 going to / visiting
6 Smoking/Advertising
7 playing   sleeping / getting to sleep
8 to have
9 to meet
10 to catch
11 to invite / to look after / to see
12 to give

10 Marketing

10.2 Ways of promoting your product

Vocabulary

2 Point of sale advertising
3 Packaging
4 Sponsorship
5 Showrooms
6 Trade fairs and exhibitions

7 Publicity
8 Public relations
9 Word of mouth
10 Telephone sales
11 Personal selling

10.3 The story of the Swatch

Listening ◎◎

Answers

True: 2 4 5 7 9 11 12
False: 1 3 6 8 10

Transcript

1st man: For three centuries the Swiss were the watch-making experts of the world. In evidence, in 1950 four out of five watches were made in Switzerland. But by 1980 this market share had dropped to one in five and by 1985 the figure was less than 5%. The Swiss watch industry was in big trouble, and they knew it. Only the luxury watch manufacturers were still making money.

Woman: Two things had led to this: technology and price. Although it was the Swiss who had invented electronic quartz watches, they were first manufactured and sold in the USA by Hamilton and Timex – these were digital watches. But by the 1970s thanks to super-efficient mass-production techniques most of these watches were made in Japan by Citizen or Seiko, or thanks to low labour costs in Hong Kong. And not in Switzerland.

2nd man: That's right, but Swiss market research showed that consumers still liked analogue watches. Now, the problem was that good ones were much more expensive than digital ones – and cheap ones were less accurate and needed winding up every day.

1st man: And there had to be a solution. The technology required to make quartz watches with hands that moved around a face was developed in Switzerland by an old watch-making company, ETA. But to make such watches at a competitive price would require huge investment – investment in a computerized production line and this was at a time when the market was all but saturated with cheap digital watches.

2nd man: So ETA took the risk of developing an unrepairable watch which was welded into a plastic case that would only cost 15 Swiss Francs to manufacture – but which would retail for considerably more. Now their innovative idea was that the new watch would be a fashion item, not an upmarket timepiece like Rolex or Omega that rich people bought to last them a lifetime. The design of the face of the watch and the strap were what would make fashionable, trendy and sporty young people want to buy what they called a *Swatch* (or preferably more than one) to wear.

The new *Swatches* wouldn't compete with cheap digital watches on price. No, they would be more expensive but much more attractive. This was going to be a completely new product.

Woman: It was such a novel product that ETA knew they needed to spend huge amounts on promotion and advertising. In 1985 they spent 30 million Swiss Francs in the USA alone

on advertising – to create a fresh, young, sporty image for the product. They spent millions on sponsoring sportspeople and sports events. Even Princess Diana wore *Swatches*. They constantly produced new designs, including *Swatches* smelling of mint, strawberry and banana.

2nd man: So, ETA made sure that the watches were not discounted by any distributor, and to maintain a demand for *Swatches*, they restricted their production so that each design was a 'Special Edition' which might hopefully become a collectible, not just a mass-produced object. The quality was excellent: the watches weren't repairable, but they didn't need to be because they didn't go wrong. Each new design was both original and fashionable.

1st man: And that was how the *Swatch* earned its place in marketing history. And how the Swiss watch-making industry was rescued by courageous investment, Swiss efficiency and innovation.

10.4 Brand names

Reading

1 cheaper expensive recession   2 label   3 vulgar/distasteful/wrong   4 Up-market/Luxury/Expensive/Designer cheap/cheaper/down-market   5 popularity/market share   6 80 great/marked/large   7 fewer   8 better

10.5 'Think marketing'

Vocabulary

20

1 l e a f l e t s
2 l a b e l
3 l a u n c h
4 c h a r t
5 c o n s u m e r
6 g r a p h
7 p o s t e r
8 d i s p l a y
9 t r a d e m a r k s
10 b a r g a i n
11 m e d i a
12 b r a n d s
13 s u r v e y
14 d e s i g n
15 r e g i o n
16 f l u c t u a t e
17 c o m p e t i t o r s
18 a d v e r t i s e d
19 c h a i n s t o r e

10.6 Prepositions – 6

2 wasting ... on
3 take into consideration
4 submit ... to
5 withdraw from
6 superior to

7 share ... with
8 specializes in
9 valid for
10 take over from

10.7 Comparing and contrasting

A

2 Red
3 silver (ones)   Blue   Black/Yellow/etc.
4 gold   Gold
5 Yellow
6 Brown   Brown
7 black   black
8 green   yellow/gold   yellow/blue/etc.

B 1

2 More cars are manufactured in Japan *than* any other country.
3 *Far more / Many more* cars are made in Germany than in Russia.
4 Japan is *the* largest manufacturer of cars in the world.
5 3 million *fewer* cars are made in Spain than in Germany.
6 About half as many cars are produced in Italy *as* in France.

2 *Suggested answers*

1 The USA produces far more cars than the UK.
  The USA produces more than four times as many cars as the UK.
2 South Korea produces (exactly) the same number of cars as the UK.
3 Mexico produces far fewer cars than Germany.
4 Germany is the third largest manufacturer of cars in the world.

C

2 All the other products are more expensive than ours.
3 There aren't as many competing brands on the market as there were ten years ago.
4 Three times as many consumers prefer our product to theirs.
5 The least important feature of the product is its colour.
6 The price is just as important as the design to our customers.
7 Their product costs a little more than ours does.
8 Our product is far more attractive than theirs.
9 It isn't quite as easy to service the new model as the old one.
10 Our product is more reliable than theirs.
11 Most of the competing brands are less widely available than our product.
12 Quality is more important than price, as far as our customers are concerned.

11 Meetings

11.2 Choose the best summary

The best summaries are: 2 b   3 a   4 b   5 c

Transcript

1 *Mr Green:* Er...if I could come in here . . .
  Chairman: Yes, Mr Green?
  Mr Green: I'd just like to say that the targets that Jim suggests would be unacceptable to my people. I mean, I can't see that a level of 4,500 is realistic. I'm sure Ms White would agree.
  Ms White: Well, no actually it seems to me that 4.5 thousand for the year is quite easily achievable. We had a 22% increase in turnover last quarter, after all. I think the others would agree with that.
  Others: Mmm! Oh yes.

2 *Miss Grey:* I'd say that the important thing for us to agree on first is the colours we'll be offering in the new product range. There's a contradiction between the reports we've been getting from our marketing interviews and from what Mr Brown suggests. The people we talked to found both the orange and yellow prototypes very appealing. I'd like to know why Mr Brown thinks that we should stick to last year's colours.
  Chairman: Mr Brown?
  Mr Brown: I resent the tone of Miss Grey's question there. She seems to think that interviews with potential customers should govern our entire policy when it comes to colour. It's well known that tastes change very rapidly when it comes to this aspect of a product. My suggestion is based on 23 years in this business and I think I know what I'm talking about. Besides, manufacturing the product in two new colours would increase our production costs by approximately $4\frac{1}{2}$%.
  Miss Grey: I see, I didn't realize that.
  Chairman: All right, well let's leave it there, shall we?

3 *Mr Black:* If we're going to spend that much on promotional literature, we need to make sure we're getting a good quality product.
  Mrs Scarlet: How do you mean, Mr Black?
  Mr Black: Well, Mrs Scarlet, the leaflets we've had done so far have been designed by our own publicity department. And quite frankly, they don't look professional enough.
  Mrs Scarlet: I think they've been doing quite a good job. And do you have any idea how much contracting this out would cost?
  Mr Black: Well, no I don't, but maybe we should find out.
  Chairman: Mrs Scarlet, would you be prepared to do that?
  Mrs Scarlet: But . . .Yes. All right.
  Chairman: Fine, next . . .

4 *Ms Pink:* I think staff training should take preference in this case.
  Chairman: Yes, well, thank you, Ms Pink. Mr Gold you don't agree?
  Mr Gold: No, not at all. In my experience, staff training is just an excuse for time-wasting. If anyone needs to find out anything they can do that on the job, when they need to.
  Ms Pink: All right, with new documentation procedures, that may be true but half the staff in your section have no idea how the computer works.
  Mr Gold: They know as much as they need to know.

Ms Pink: But if they knew more, they could make it work for them instead of regarding it as a piece of technical equipment.

Mr Gold: We could give it a try, I suppose.

Chairman: Well, perhaps you could draw up some guidelines, Ms Pink?

5 *Chairman:* Yes, Mr Dark?

Mr Dark: I'd like to raise a point about office services.

Chairman: Yes.

Mr Dark: As you all know, we have a big turnover of staff in our section. And a number of our new staff have come to me very upset recently. I had one girl in tears yesterday. The problem is that if they want someone in office services to do anything for them, they have to know exactly who to ask. I mean, it's easy for the old hands – they've learnt who's in charge of what. But if you approach the wrong person there, you just get a sarcastic or a superior answer and no help at all. I think that Mrs Bright should talk to her people and tell them to be more considerate. And it would be a big help if she should draw up a clear handout explaining who is responsible for what. It's just not fair, otherwise.

Ms Bright: Goodness, I think you're over-reacting, Mr Dark. It was probably Shirley or Ted again. But if you think it'll help I'll have a word with them. Once you get to know them they're very nice, they just seem fierce. And we already have a handout like the one you describe. If you haven't got a copy, I'll send you one.

Mr Dark: Thank you, Ms Bright.

11.3 About this meeting ...

Listening & note-taking 🎧

Model messages

To Mr Hanson

Ingrid Muster called from Berlin.
Problem with flights: won't arrive till Friday 2.30.
Apologies but unavoidable. But meeting can continue in evening. Please inform your people.
She's bringing Peter – he's done all the research, so best person to put everyone in picture.
Please book 2 rooms at the Royal Hotel for night of 13th and cancel booking for night of 12th.

To Linda Taylor

Tim Hanson called re meeting on Friday 13th.
Time changed because Ingrid can't get flight from Berlin.
New time: 2.30 instead of 10.30. But lunch is still on and you're welcome to join them. Please call Mrs Burrows on 345 0982 to confirm whether joining them for lunch or not.
Meeting will go on at least till 6, probably longer, so you may need to book hotel room. You can do this or call Mrs Burrows to do this for you. (Ingrid and Peter staying at Royal, near station. If full, Imperial nearby is good.)
Any problems, call Mrs Burrows. Or call Mr Hanson at home this evening on 778 8021.

Transcript

Ingrid Muster: This is Ingrid Muster (INGRID MUSTER) calling from Berlin. Can you tell Mr Hanson that I've had a problem with flights. The one I was going to book on is full – there's a big football match on apparently. So, the earliest I can make it on Friday is 2.30. I'm sorry about this, but there's nothing I can do. It does mean we can continue the

meeting as long as we like into the evening, though. Can you let your people know, please? I know that Linda has to travel down from Glasgow that day – at least she won't have to set off quite so early. The other thing is, I'd like to bring Peter with me, if that's all right, yes? He's done all the research on this project, so he's really the best person to put everyone into the picture. Can you book us both into the Royal Hotel for the night of the 13th and cancel my booking for the night of the 12th?

Tim Hanson: Hello, this is Tim Hanson. I'd like you to give a message to Linda Taylor about the meeting on Friday the 13th. The thing is we've had to change it because Ingrid can't get a flight from Berlin. So the new time is 2.30 instead of 10.30. But the lunch is still on and Linda is welcome to join us for that – if she wants to. Could she call Mrs Burrows (BURROWS) on 345 0982 to confirm whether she will be joining us for lunch or not. Ah, and the meeting will go on at least till 6, probably longer, so maybe Linda will need to book a hotel room. She can do this herself, or again, she could call Mrs Burrows to do this for her. Ingrid and Peter are staying at the Royal, near the station. If that's full, the er...the Imperial nearby is good. If there are any problems, call Mrs Burrows. Or you can get me at home this evening on 778 8021. OK?

11.4 At ... and by ...

Prepositional phrases – 1

2 at last
3 by accident
4 at a loss
5 at least
6 at cost price
7 at a bargain price
8 by fax
9 by letter
10 at our expense
11 at a good price
12 at a profit
13 by air
14 at your disposal
15 by return of post/mail

11.5 Decision-making

Vocabulary

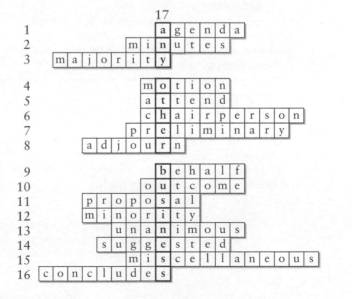

17

1   a g e n d a
2   m i n u t e s
3   m a j o r i t y
4   m o t i o n
5   a t t e n d
6   c h a i r p e r s o n
7   p r e l i m i n a r y
8   a d j o u r n
9   b e h a l f
10 o u t c o m e
11 p r o p o s a l
12 m i n o r i t y
13 u n a n i m o u s
14 s u g g e s t e d
15 m i s c e l l a n e o u s
16 c o n c l u d e s

11.6 Suffixes – 2 *Word-building*

debtor distributor examiner inspector insurer
inventor investigator manufacturer negotiator
operator purchaser retailer shipper supplier
wholesaler

payee licensee consignee

to categorize   to computerize   to privatize
to nationalize   to legalize   to generalize   to subsidize
to specialize   to rationalize   to modernize

tighten loosen harden brighten flatten sharpen
sweeten

11.7 Games people play at meetings
Reading

True: 1 3 5 6 9
False: 2 4 (six roles are mentioned) 7 8 10

11.8 *A, an, the* and *Ø*   *Grammar review*

2 The trouble with ~~the~~ large meetings is that they go on
  for *a* longer time than small ones.
3 You have to catch *the/a* train from ~~the~~ Paddington
  Station to get to Wales.
4 She's a student and she's studying ~~the~~ economics at ~~the~~
  Vienna Technical University.
5 I'm staying in ~~the~~ room number 609 at *the* Holiday Inn
  near the airport.
6 ~~The~~ most of my colleagues are more interested in ~~the~~
  sport than in business.
7 Could you give me ~~an~~ *some* information about the
  venue of *the* meeting?
8 Does the machine need *a* new component or do we
  need to think about ordering ~~a~~ new equipment?
9 I sometimes get *the/a* feeling that I spend all my time in
  ~~the~~ meetings.
10 I don't enjoy talking on ~~a~~ *the* phone, I prefer to send a
   fax or write ~~the~~ letters. / *a letter.*

1 More and more, shoppers are by-passing (the) household names
  for the cheaper no-name products one shelf over. This shows
  that even the biggest and strongest brands in the world are
  vulnerable.
2 The larger the meeting, the longer it may take to reach a
  decision. There seem to be ideal sizes for meetings, depending
  on the purpose. A meeting where information is being given to
  people can be quite large, because there is not likely to be
  much discussion and questions may be asked by a few
  individuals on everyone else's behalf.

3 Even one-to-one or small informal meetings are structured
  (usually with an agenda) and planned. They are different from
  chance conversations in the corridor or over coffee. Small
  informal meetings may also take place or continue during a
  meal.
4 All meetings have one thing in common: role-playing. The most
  formal role is that of (the) chairman. He (and it is usually a he)
  sets the agenda, and a good chairman will keep the/a meeting
  running on time and to the point. Sadly, (the) other, informal
  role-players are often able to gain the upper hand. Chief is the
  "constant talker", who just loves to hear his or her own voice.

12 Processes and operations

12.2 Doing things *Vocabulary*

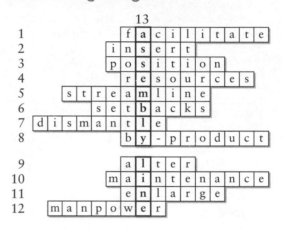

12.3 Explaining *Functions & listening*

A *Suggested answers*

2 'All you have to do is press this button. OK?'
3 'That's clear, is it?'
4 'Make sure you remember to . . .'
5 'I wonder if I might trouble you for a moment?'
6 'Sorry to bother you, but . . .'
7 'How do you do that again?'
8 'I'm sorry, could you explain that part again?'

B

1 Using a personal computer
2 Making a paper aeroplane
3 Starting a record player
4 Typing a report

Transcript

1 First of all you have to put the plug in. And be careful not to
  forget to take the covers off. Now you first switch this on
  here and also you switch this on. Now I take one of these
  and push it into this slot. Like this. Is that clear? It only takes
  a few seconds to load. And then I can select what I'm going
  to be working on. Right, then I click this little thing on here.
  You see that arrow? And then the whole thing starts up. And
  now I'm ready for serious work. When I've finished whatever
  job I've been doing, I have to take care to save it like this.

Answer Key and Transcripts

Then I take this out and put it away and then I can use another one of these and repeat the same general procedure, leaving it on all the while.

2 You take a piece of paper. A4 size will do. First you fold it all the way down the middle. And then unfold the corners at one end. Then you fold in the corners so that they meet the original crease. Now fold in the new edges so that they meet the centre crease. And then fold once again to meet the centre crease. Next, fold the point to meet the side edge. Now comes the tricky bit. Fold the edge twice, to give it some weight. And then make a double fold. Then you need a pair of scissors. You need to cut out a small section not far back from the nose and fold down the wings. Now to throw it you need to hook an average size rubber band in the cut-out section and grasp the end. Stretch back and let go. I hope you have fun with it.

3 First of all make sure the machine is plugged in. And then switched on. We then open it up here and, by the way, don't forget to move the control arm clear. Take what you want to hear out of the sleeve and place it on the spindle. At this stage you may have to check that the correct speed has been selected. If not, of course, you have to select it. Then switch the control to automatic. And as long as the thing is on, that's it. Just lean back and enjoy it.

4 Now to start off with you use A4 paper. OK? You have to make one top copy and then two extra copies. And you should type in double spacing on one side of the paper only. OK? Now you have to leave a 40 millimetre margin on the left-hand side. About 25 millimetres at the right. And 25 millimetres at the top and the bottom. Don't type part of a word on one line and then part of it on the next, please. And don't type a hyphen at the end or the start of a line. Now number the pages in the centre of each page at the top. Use a separate page for each of the tables. All right. The number of the table and the heading should be immediately above the table. Don't indent the first paragraph after a heading. Don't underline the headings. Only underline the words that are underlined in the manuscript. And finally, the contents page is to be typed last, when the page numbers are known.

12.4 In ... *Prepositional phrases – 2*

2 in progress
3 in accordance with
4 in bulk
5 in advance
6 in transit
7 in consultation with
8 in confidence
9 in charge of
10 in debt

12.5 Anti-noise *Listening*

A

☑ Anti-noise creates vibrations which affect sound waves.

B

1 c 2 b 3 a 4 a 5 c 6 b 7 c

Transcript

Interviewer: Now, turning to the problem of noise – what can we do to fight the increasing huge volumes of noise affecting us all today, like the noise you can hear in the background in this factory we're standing in now? I have with me Dr Susan Hall, one of North America's leading experts on what is called 'anti-noise'. Dr Hall, what can be done?

Dr Hall: Well, strange though it may sound to you, one of the best ways to make machinery quieter, like in cars, for example, may be to make it noisier.

Interviewer: Really?

Dr Hall: Yes, the source of this paradox is electronic 'anti-noise', which creates sound waves to combat unwanted rattles, blare and thumping. Now although the idea dates back to the 1930s, it's only recently that advances in computer technology have made 'anti-noise' a commercial possibility.

Interviewer: And where has this happened?

Dr Hall: Well, America.

Interviewer: Huhuh.

Dr Hall: Here industry spends a fortune to get rid of noise. We all know how unpleasant it is. Delicate machinery is interfered with and people working in factories and ordinary people at home enjoying their leisure can be affected by noise.

Interviewer: Yes.

Dr Hall: Even very, very small vibrations can cause parts to wear out and equipment to fail. And this is very important, all this gets added on to the price of the product. Did you know that about five to fifteen per cent of the price of a product comes from noise and vibration costs? But the usual methods used to dampen down noise and vibration rely on techniques that are thirty to forty years old.

Interviewer: And what are they?

Dr Hall: Well, these usually involve wrapping or covering the noisy or vibrating component with anything from cotton to concrete. But it's often very expensive and very inefficient. The performance of the noisy part also suffers as a result. Well, this is the case with the car muffler or silencer.

Interviewer: And how does this differ from these new techniques?

Dr Hall: The modern electronic 'anti-noise' devices don't muffle. Instead, sound is used to attack sound.

Interviewer: And how do you do that?

Dr Hall: Well, the trick is to hit these sound waves with other waves in a carefully controlled way. It may not be possible to eliminate noise completely, but engineers can build systems to eliminate specific kinds of noise and vibration. The new systems can deal with repetitive noise. This unfortunately means that there is not much that can be done about unpredictable noises like someone trying to play the trumpet . . .

But they can handle fairly regular things like engine cylinders or the sound of a turbine turning around. One new technique involves the use of a microphone and a microprocessor. The processor measures the sound and directs a loudspeaker to broadcast sound waves that are a hundred and eighty degrees out of phase with the engine noise. The developers claim that it would make a car engine quieter and more efficient, if not one hundred per cent silent.

Interviewer: Aren't there other areas of application in the noisy industrial environment of today? I mean, we're all of us affected in some way or another.

Dr Hall: True.

Interviewer: Whether we work in a noisy factory or not.

Dr Hall: Sure. One system which the same company is developing aims to minimize the noise of aircraft engines and helicopter vibrations. The design of new aircraft engines today means that they're often more fuel efficient than earlier ones. But they're also noisier. 'Anti-noise' systems would be able to reduce noise in the cabin of an aircraft to more acceptable levels.

Interviewer: That's brilliant. And how about the noisy workplace? And the effect on the workers themselves?

Dr Hall: Sure. Well, people working in noisy workplaces are probably more affected by noise than anything else. 'Anti-noise' techniques can create zones of quiet in loud workplaces – well, like the one we're standing in now. You can hear the factory noise all around you, but we can still carry on a conversation without having to shout, can't we?

Interviewer: Yes, but how does this work?

Dr Hall: Well, to create a zone, microphones are suspended around a work station on a factory floor. Loudspeakers that generate out of phase sound waves are put close to the worker under the desk or the workbench. Well, there's one, look, over there. Yeah, yeah. And the rest of the factory remains noisy. If we just step outside the zone, you'll hear what I mean.

Interviewer: OK, let's try that. Here we go . . .

Dr Hall: See what I mean?

Interviewer: Yes, let's get back inside the quiet zone, shall we?

12.6 About time

Reading

1 more quickly/rapidly/fast   2 steps/tasks sequence/order
3 Queues bottlenecks/delays/hold-ups   4 flexible/efficient
5 smaller large   6 invest respond   7 fashions/trends
8 standardised runs/numbers

12.7 Modal verbs

Grammar review

2 The firm could build the car at this plant.
3 That could/may be why the company closed down.
4 We might/may enlarge the present site.
5 They may use this canteen.
6 You must follow the instructions closely.
7 They ought to / should pay more for overtime.
8 The assembly line doesn't have to stop / needn't stop for them to do the maintenance work.
9 You must have experience for this job.
10 We can't help you this time.

2 d   3 f   4 e   5 c   6 h   7 b   8 g

---

13 Jobs and careers

13.2 Who should we short-list?

Listening & note-taking ◎◎

Suggested answers

REPORT FROM:	GUS MORRISON IN GLASGOW
Best candidate:	**Duncan McCabe** Age: 21
Education:	Graduate of Edinburgh University (MA in modern languages)
Languages:	Speaks fluent French and quite good German
Work experience:	Publicity department of Glasgow City Council (about a year)
Personality:	Very pleasant, a bit shy when you first talk to him, but when you get to know him he has a lovely sense of humour
Availability:	Not available until September 1st
Suitability:	Very bright and eager and he'd fit in well with your people down in London
Address:	145 Pentland Gardens, Glasgow, G5 8TG
Phone:	041 667 8092

REPORT FROM:	LAURA STEELE IN SHEFFIELD
Best candidate:	**Mrs Sylvia Sabbatini** Age: 25
Education:	Paper qualifications not all that good: left school at 16 to do secretarial course
Languages:	Speaks Italian fluently (father Italian, mother English)
Work experience:	Johnson Brothers in Marketing since leaving school
Personality:	Lovely personality – very cheerful and bright
Availability:	Husband has just got a job in London, so able to start work in London right away
Suitability:	Very intelligent young woman – she impressed me very much
Address:	78 Pennine Avenue, Huddersfield, LS34 7QT
Phone:	0484 078432

REPORT FROM:	TERRY WILLIAMS IN CARDIFF
Best candidate:	**Miss Emma Harris** Age: 20
Education:	Had right exam results to get into university, but decided to go into industry
Languages:	Speaks Spanish and French (not exactly fluent, but so confident this doesn't matter)
Work experience:	Working in marketing for small light engineering firm, had become Export Marketing Manager. Firm taken over and she was made redundant – they decided to close her department
Personality:	Full of confidence, makes friends easily
Availability:	No ties here, could start work next week if you wanted
Suitability:	Has really good potential – would work well in a team
Address:	214 Gower Road, Swansea, SA2 4PJ
Phone:	0792 98762

Transcript

Gus Morrison: Good afternoon. This is Gus Morrison calling from Glasgow. Now, most of the people I've talked to today have been pretty hopeless. One of them was obviously lying when he filled in the application form. Do you know, he claimed to speak German, but when I started talking to him in German, he couldn't understand!

Well, now, the best of the bunch was er...where is it...er Duncan McCabe (that's D-U-N-C-A-N M-c-C-A-B-E). He's quite young, he's only 21 and he's a graduate of Edinburgh...Edinburgh University. He's got an MA and it's in modern languages. Now, he's been working for the publicity department of Glasgow City Council for about a year. He speaks fluent French and his German is quite good too. He's a very pleasant lad, he seems a bit shy when you first talk to him, but when you get to know him he's got a lovely sense of humour, and I think he's very bright, he's very eager and I think he'd fit in well with your people down in London. Now unfortunately he's not available until September 1st.

But if you want to contact him, his address is 145 Pentland (I'll spell that, that's P-E-N-T-L-A-N-D) Pentland Gardens, Glasgow, and the postcode is G5 8TG, and his phone number is 041 667 8092.

Laura Steele: Hello, this is Laura Steele, I'm calling from Sheffield. I've spent this morning interviewing four candidates and the best one is a Mrs Sylvia Sabbatini (that's S-Y-L-V-I-A S-A-B-B-A-T-I-N-I). Now, she's 25, she's married and has been working for Johnson Brothers, in Marketing since leaving school. She has a lovely personality – very cheerful and bright. She speaks Italian fluently (her father is Italian, her mother is English). Her qualifications on paper are not all that good, she left school at 16 to do a secretarial course, but she's a very intelligent young woman – she impressed me very much. She's been married for two years, no children, and her husband has just got a job in London, so she'd be able to start work in London more or less right away.

Her address is 78 Pennine Avenue, Pennine (P-E-N-N-I-N-E) Avenue, Huddersfield (that's H-U-D-D-E-R-S-F-I-E-L-D), and the postcode is LS34 7QT. Her telephone number is 0484 078432.

Terry Williams: Hello, this is Terry Williams calling from Cardiff. I've just finished a very frustrating day interviewing people for you. There were really only two applicants that you should have invited for interview and I discovered after half an hour that one of them isn't available: he'd already accepted another job but decided to come to the interview anyway!

So the only person I have to tell you about is Miss Emma Harris (that's E-M-M-A H-A-R-R-I-S). She's only 20 but she has really good potential. She had all the right exam results to get into university when she left school, but decided to go into industry. She speaks Spanish and French, though she's not exactly fluent in either, but she's so confident I don't think that matters.

She's been working in marketing for a small light engineering firm and she had just become their Export Marketing Manager when the firm was taken over and she was made redundant because they decided to close her department. She is full of confidence, makes friends easily and she would work well in a team. She has no ties here, and she could start next week if you wanted. I think she'd be a real find and you should get in touch with her right away.

Her address is 214 Gower Road (that's G-O-W-E-R), Swansea (S-W-A-N-S-E-A), SA2 4PJ. Her phone number is 0792 98762. All right. Ah, cheerio then.

13.3 Abstract nouns

Word-building

Ⓐ ②

acknowledgement achievement agreement announcement arrangement development endorsement judgement measurement repayment

adaptation alteration application authorization cancellation centralization confirmation consultation declaration determination devaluation imagination modification recommendation specialization

appreciation arbitration calculation collaboration co-operation elimination fluctuation integration location speculation

attraction collection contribution correction deduction deletion interruption pollution prediction protection reduction

Ⓑ ②

calmness carelessness cheapness friendliness helpfulness lateness loudness seriousness

confidence intelligence patience difference

capability flexibility formality possibility probability popularity reality reliability scarcity sincerity

13.4 Have a nice day

Reading

1 paid unrewarding/dull 2 turnover 3 survey keep 4 appreciated 5 loyal well/highly not 6 third

13.5 Employment

Vocabulary

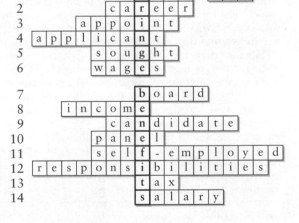

1. fill out (15)
2. career
3. appoint
4. applicant
5. sought
6. wages
7. board
8. income
9. candidate
10. panel
11. self-employed
12. responsibilities
13. tax
14. salary

13.6 On ...

Prepositional phrases – 3

2 on display	10 on business
3 on the spot	11 on vacation/on holiday
4 on request	12 on condition
5 on order	13 on paper
6 on closer inspection	14 on loan
7 on the phone	15 on behalf of
8 on approval	16 on schedule
9 on time	

13.7 High-flyers

Listening

Presenter: 1 c 2 a 3 a
Rod Scott: 4 b 5 c 6 c
Heather Stewart: 7 b 8 b 9 c 10 c 11 b 12 b

Transcript

Presenter: . . . the first high-flyer schemes were introduced in the 1960s and now many sectors of commerce, industry and the civil service pick out their most promising younger managers as 'high-flyers'. You find schemes of this kind mostly in large companies or groups of companies, where the fairly rigid career structure can only be broken by by-passing the normal steps in the promotion ladder.

It can take a company many years to develop a top-level manager, if he or she joins them straight from university. Such people must obtain wide experience in different parts of the company and this can take up to 20 years. This means that someone who joins the firm from university works for the company in different capacities, and is identified as a high-flyer, can expect to reach top management at around the age of 40.

Rod Scott has been looking at what is called the 'individual development programme' at BP.

Rod Scott: BP is one of the largest multinational companies in the world. It employs 130,000 people. It has 260 managers involved in its own 'individual development programme' who will compete for 180 senior positions in the group. They don't join the scheme until they are in their late 20s, by which time they will have established themselves in their special field, they will have built up their professional reputation and they will have a record of high performance. While they're on the scheme (and this lasts 5 to 10 years) their progress is supervised by a committee of 15 senior managers. One of the main purposes of the scheme is to provide them with experience outside their own field – in finance, working in an overseas division, or experience in information technology.

Presenter: But high-flyer schemes have their drawbacks, according to Heather Stewart, a management consultant.

Heather Stewart: One weakness is that you may be creating a management team who think and act in the same ways. That means, if your business changes, they may not be able to meet the challenges. As outsiders tend to be excluded as senior recruits, the company may be cutting itself off from a pool of talent which their competitors can draw on. Another problem is that late-starters are also excluded – not everyone is at their peak in their 20s and such qualities as experience and in-depth knowledge may be undervalued.

Another weakness is that women are often excluded from high-flyer schemes, since schemes identify high-flyers at the very time when women are most likely to have children: they are forced to choose between career and family.

Worst of all though is the resentment that high-flyers create among other managers who aren't chosen to be high-flyers. Developing a sort of élite, a chosen few, within an organization is quite simply bad for company morale – it makes everyone else feel they are being undervalued and takes away their enthusiasm and dedication – and clearly this is counter-productive. This is particularly noticeable in medium-sized companies, where high-flyer schemes seem to be particularly controversial and divisive. There have been various experiments . . .

13.8 Relative clauses

Grammar review

B *Suggested answers* Notice that commas are not required in sentences 2, 3, 6 and 9.

2 An interviewer who tries to frighten the candidate is abusing his/her superior position.
3 On the other hand, an interview which is too relaxed and friendly may not find out how a candidate reacts to stress.
4 My friend Nick, who feels very nervous at interviews, finds it hard to put himself over.
5 A handwritten letter, which many companies prefer to a typed one, can show the reader more of your personality than a typed one.
6 A CV which gives too much information may not be read carefully.
7 Your curriculum vitae, which you should always send a copy of, is a document you can use over and over again.
8 Your application for the post, which was mailed on 4 May, did not arrive till after the deadline for applications.
9 Unfortunately, the envelope in which your documents were sent contained your letter and photograph, but not your CV.
10 Mrs Mary O'Farrell, with whom you have been corresponding, is no longer working with our firm.

C Notice that commas are not required in sentences 7 and 8.

2 Mr Wright, whose application form we received yesterday, is a very promising candidate.
3 His CV, which you showed me yesterday, is most impressive.
4 He has excellent references from his present employers, who are ACME Engineering.
5 He was working in Norwich, where they have their HQ.
6 His qualifications, which you commented on, are excellent.
7 The personnel officer who interviewed him says that he's available at once.
8 The thing that impressed her most is his personality.

D Notice that commas are only required in sentences 4 and 6.

2 I heard about the vacancy from a friend who works in Personnel.
3 She gave me some information that/which was supposed to be confidential.

4 I heard about this from a colleague, who assured me it was true.
5 Apparently, we sent the forms to an address which/that was wrong.
6 I had to fill in a six-page application form, which was very time-consuming.
7 I applied for a job that/which I saw advertised in the newspaper.
8 The person whose name you gave as a reference is unwilling to comment on you.

14 Sales and negotiation

14.2 Of, out of ...
Prepositional phrases – 4

2 of minor importance
3 of inferior quality
4 out of order
5 out of work
6 out of date
7 With reference to
8 of short duration
9 to a certain extent
10 out of stock

14.3 Asking for and giving advice
Functions & listening ⊚⊚

B

2 c 3 e 4 f 5 b 6 b 7 c 8 a 9 d 10 a

C *Suggested answers*

Conversation 1
1 They're on first name terms. Friends.
2 The woman says she's not sure what to do now she has just got the sack.
3 The man suggests she ought to look through the adverts in the newspaper or that she could perhaps start up her own business.
4 We don't know.

Conversation 2
1 Colleagues at work.
2 One woman wonders what she should do because her boss has asked her out to dinner.
3 The second woman advises her to ring up the boss's wife and tell her about it.
4 Yes.

Conversation 3
1 Colleagues.
2 One woman wonders what she should do about the constant lateness of the girl in her office.
3 The other woman says she could talk to the girl about it.
4 Yes.

Transcript

Conversation 1
Man: You look a bit worried, Monica. Is anything wrong?
Woman: No, not really.
Man: Sure? You're not really looking your normal cheerful self today.
Woman: Well, to tell you the truth, I've just been given the sack.
Man: My goodness! I...you poor thing! Oh dear me!
Woman: Well, it's my own fault really. I lost my temper with the boss and told him to go to hell. But now I'm not sure what to do.
Man: Well, if I were you, I'd start looking through the situations vacant columns in the newspaper.
Woman: But don't you think I'll find it difficult to get another job?
Man: Not for a person with your experience and qualifications. No, no, you'll have no problems.
Woman: But might it not be a good idea to move to another city?
Man: True. Have you, er, ever thought of starting up your own business?

Conversation 2
1st woman: Deborah, I'd appreciate your advice on a problem I've got.
2nd woman: Certainly, Marilyn, let's hear it.
1st woman: Well, you know I'm Mr Burlington's personal secretary?
2nd woman: Yes.
1st woman: Well, he's asked me to have dinner with him. Must be the third time he's asked in the past month. What should I do?
2nd woman: He's married, isn't he?
1st woman: Yes, he is. And he's got three small children, as well.
2nd woman: Well, if I were you, I'd just ring his wife up and tell her.
1st woman: Really?
2nd woman: There's nothing he'll be able to do, is there? He'll be so shocked.
1st woman: That sounds a great idea! Thanks, I'll try it.

Conversation 3
1st woman: What ought I to do about the girl I share an office with?
2nd woman: Why? What's the matter?
1st woman: You see, she's constantly coming late. I have to make excuses for her not being in the office when people ring up. And I also have to make up stories to hide the fact from her boss.
2nd woman: Oh, I see.
1st woman: I mean, I like her. And we actually get on very well together. But it's got so bad that it's beginning to make me ill.
2nd woman: Oh dear. Well, if it's so serious, why don't you invite her round to my place one evening and we can have a drink together. And I can talk to her about it. What do you think about that?
1st woman: That sounds a good idea. Oh, would you? I'd be so grateful to you, if you would.
2nd woman: Of course.

14.4 Talking shop   *Vocabulary*

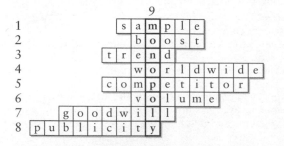

1 s a m p l e
2 b o o s t
3 t r e n d
4 w o r l d w i d e
5 c o m p e t i t o r
6 v o l u m e
7 g o o d w i l l
8 p u b l i c i t y

14.5 Co-operation and competition   *Reading*

1 facts/subject policy personal people 2 attitude
3 people problem language 4 co-operative interests
relationship concessions 5 competitive opponents one-
off hostile threatening 6 blend/mixture linguistic/verbal
non-verbal 7 facts people competition co-operation

14.6 International styles of negotiating
Listening

A Points mentioned: 1   4

B According to the speaker …

Americans are direct – even blunt
Americans are informal and open
Brazilians look people straight in the eyes
Brazilians make points in an indirect way
British are pragmatic and down to earth
British hold negotiations up
French are ordered and organized
French negotiate from a rational and clearly defined
  position
Germans are very well prepared
Germans can appear direct and uncompromising
Japanese are extremely polite
Japanese choose their words very carefully
Spaniards are thought of as pushy, even aggressive
Swedes are distant
Swedes are indirect, even evasive

Transcript

Interviewer: I'm talking to Jane Crockett who has spent many
  years negotiating for several well-known national and
  multinational companies. Hello, Jane.
Crockett: Hello.
Interviewer: Now Jane, you've experienced and observed the
  negotiation strategies used by people from different countries
  and speakers of different languages. So, before we come on to
  the differences, could I ask you to comment first of all on
  what such encounters have in common?
Crockett: OK, well, I'm just going to focus on the situations
  where people speak English in international business
  situations.
Interviewer: I see. Now not everyone speaks English to the
  same degree of proficiency. So maybe that affects the
  situation?
Crockett: Yes, perhaps. But that's not always so significant.
  Well, because, I mean, negotiations between business partners

from different countries normally mean that we have
negotiations between individuals who belong to distinct
cultural traditions.
Interviewer: Oh, I see.
Crockett: Well, every individual has a different way of
  performing various tasks in everyday life.
Interviewer: Yes, but, but isn't it the case that in a business
  negotiation they must come together and work together, to a
  certain extent? Doesn't that level out the style of…the style
  differences somewhat?
Crockett: Oh, I'm not so sure. I mean, there are people in the
  so-called Western world who say that in the course of the
  past 30 or 40 years that a lot of things have changed a great
  deal globally. And that as a consequence national differences
  have diminished or have got fewer, giving way to some sort
  of international Americanized style.
Interviewer: Yeah, I've heard that. Now some people say that
  this Americanized style has acted as a model for local
  patterns.
Crockett: Maybe it has, maybe it hasn't. Because, on the one
  hand, there does appear to be a fairly unified, even uniform
  style of doing business, with certain basic principles and
  preferences – you know, like 'time is money'. But at the same
  time it's very important to remember that we all retain
  aspects of our national characteristics – but it is actually
  behaviour that we're talking about here. We shouldn't be too
  quick to generalize that to national characteristics and
  stereotypes. It doesn't help much.
Interviewer: Yeah, you mentioned Americanized style. What is
  particular about the American style of business bargaining or
  negotiating?
Crockett: Well, I've noticed that, for example, when Americans
  negotiate with people from Brazil, the American negotiators
  make their points in a direct self-explanatory way. While the
  Brazilians make points in a more indirect way. Brazilian
  importers, for example, look the people they're talking to
  straight in the eyes a lot. They spend time on what for some
  people seems to be background information. They seem to be
  more indirect. An American conversation style, on the other
  hand, is far more like that of point-making: first point,
  second point, third point, and so on. Now of course, this isn't
  the only way in which one can negotiate. And there's
  absolutely no reason why this should be considered the best
  way to negotiate.
Interviewer: Right. Americans seem to have a different style,
  say, even from the British, don't they?
Crockett: Exactly. Which just shows how careful you must be
  about generalizing. I mean, how else can you explain how
  American negotiators are perceived as informal and
  sometimes much too open? For in British eyes Americans are
  direct – even blunt. And at the same time, for the British too,
  German negotiators can appear direct and uncompromising
  in negotiations. And yet if you experience Germans and
  Americans negotiating together it's often the Americans who
  are being too blunt for the German negotiators.
Interviewer: Fascinating. So people from different European
  countries use a different style, do they?
Crockett: N…That's right. I mean, another example which I've
  come across is the difference between Spaniards and Swedes
  in business negotiations. Now Spaniards tend to think of
  many North Europeans, such as Germans or Swedes as not
  being very outspoken – even to the point of being inhibited.
  And you sometimes even hear remarks about Swedes not
  being able to engage in personal relationships, that sort of
  thing. On the other hand, many North Europeans tend to
  think of Spaniards as pushy, or even aggressive.
  Sometimes on a personal level, Spaniards tend to

Answer Key and Transcripts

disapprove of what they interpret to be Swedish indirectness, even evasiveness. Swedes are sometimes characterized by Spaniards as being distant or cold. And not easy to get on with. Or not easy to get into personal contact with. And their behaviour in business negotiations is seen as very impersonal.

Interviewer: I've heard it said though that the British give this same impression to Spaniards.

Crockett: Well, that's true. And yet in other contexts the British tend to give the impression of not following a particular line. They try to sort of fit in with the way a negotiation is going. They're sometimes seen as pragmatic and down to earth. In contrast, say to French negotiators, who tend to have a more ordered and organized set of objectives, and when they make a contribution to the negotiation they do so from a rational and clearly defined position. They don't give the impression of wishing to move either from their opinion or their planned 'route'.

Interviewer: While the British are more flexible?

Crockett: Um…I'm not sure about that. In my experience they sometimes have the reputation of not always being fully prepared or of not being entirely clear what they want. Or even sometimes holding negotiations up, when things could move forward more smoothly. Unlike, say, their German counterparts. The Germans, well in my experience, usually tend to be very well prepared.

Interviewer: Mmm. OK…so…what about the Japanese then? I mean, is their style different from Europeans?

Crockett: Oh well, yes, of course. Many Europeans note the extreme politeness of their Japanese counterparts. The way they avoid giving the slightest offence, you know. They're also very reserved towards people they don't know well. At the first meetings, American colleagues have difficulties in finding the right approach sometimes. But then, when you meet them again, this initial impression tends to disappear. But it is perhaps true to say that your average Japanese business person does choose his, or, more rarely, her words very carefully.

Interviewer: So whatever nationalities you're dealing with, you need to remember that different nationalities negotiate in different ways.

Crockett: Well, it's perhaps more helpful to bear in mind that different people behave and negotiate in different ways – and you shouldn't assume that everyone will behave in the same way that you do . . .

14.7 Order of adverbs
Grammar review

1 The corporate headquarters **recently** moved from Houston to Charlotte.
2 The company **very quickly** realized that it was a profit-making area.
3 Our sales staff worked **hard** the whole year.
4 The machine was **carefully** serviced by the engineer.
5 The production schedule will **probably** be achieved.
6 The order book is **currently** stagnating.
7 They check their inventory **weekly**.
8 I'm sorry to say there is little we can **immediately** do.
9 The customer delivered the cargo **punctually**.
10 We have **gradually** increased our product range in order to give our customers more choice.

1 There have **rarely** been disputes with our suppliers.
2 Last year there were **frequently** delays in concluding contracts.
3 The company **nearly** went bankrupt as a result.
4 Now our firm is **probably** going to open a European factory.
5 We would **certainly** have accepted the offer.
6 Serious clients can **hardly** expect to be told the facts.
7 You **obviously** don't know what we're talking about.
8 The customers **always** complain when we send John instead of Margaret to the sales conference.
9 Their operating expenses **apparently** remained low.
10 The liaison officer **completely** forgot to inform the export manager's PA.

1 There has **definitely** been a mistake in this invoice.
2 European computer manufacturers are **apparently** going to work together on this project.
3 Do you think the firm will **ever** get the Chinese order?
4 The final price was **occasionally** much higher than the purchaser expected.
5 The customer was **initially** quite satisfied with our after-sales service.
6 We **specifically** asked to see the chief negotiator before we made the decision.
7 The CEO has **just** announced the export team for the Taiwan project.
8 We are **certainly** going to investigate the whole question as soon as possible.
9 If the correct procedure is followed you will **hardly ever** have a breakdown.
10 Although the freight was **carefully** handled, important components were broken in transit.

15 Revision

15.1 Grammar revision

1 c 2 c 3 a 4 a 5 c 6 c 7 d 8 b 9 d 10 a 11 a
12 d 13 d 14 a 15 b 16 d 17 c 18 b 19 b 20 c

15.2 Vocabulary revision

15.3 Functions revision

1 e 2 g 3 a 4 j 5 b 6 h 7 c 8 i 9 d 10 f

 Suggested answers – *many variations are possible*

1 Good morning, Mrs Martin, it's nice to see you again. Did you have a good journey?
2 Yes, certainly, you can use the phone in my office. Just dial 9 for an outside line.
3 Sorry, could you say that again, please?
4 Yes, I know, I'm very sorry about that. There was a slip-up in our shipping department.
5 Thanks for letting me know. I'll look into that right away.
6 I'm absolutely sure that our new product will sell well.
7 That's exactly what I think.
8 Well, the first thing you have to do is . . .
9 Well, if I were you, I'd place an order for 250, because . . .
10 Mrs Martin, did I ever tell you about . . . ?

15.4 Word-building revision

1 tighten
2 flexibility
3 modernization
4 inexperienced
5 oversimplification
6 unreliable
7 repayment
8 anti-clockwise
9 administrator
10 recommendation

15.5 Midway International   *Writing*

Model letters – *many variations are possible*

Midway International
P.O. Box 777   K-4550 Euroville   Yourland

Mrs J. McArthur
Original Products plc
20 Kirkton Campus
Livingston EH54 6QA
Scotland   April 10, 1999

Dear Mrs McArthur,

Our order MI/876

We were very dismayed to receive your letter of 2 April, announcing a delay in shipping this order. I should like to point out that we have customers waiting and that if the goods do not arrive soon, we shall have to cancel this order. It is essential that we receive the units by 1 May at the very latest. May I ask you to make sure that you give our order top priority, as we have been loyal customers of yours for many years.

A further point in your letter gives us great concern. You say that the speed of the unit is 'slightly reduced'. In our opinion, however, the speed of the unit is considerably slower than the specification. We fear that our customers will not find this acceptable. In view of this, we suggest that your price to us should be reduced by $45 per unit.

Regarding feedback on your OP 424 series, we will ask our own customers for their comments and keep you informed. We have one OP 424 in our head office which does seem to overheat, but so far this unit has not broken down – yet!

We would also like to know whether, in case of breakdown, users should return the defective units directly to your factory for repair or replacement.

We look forward to hearing from you and hope that you can reassure us on the points made above.

Yours sincerely,
Your name
p.p. M. Meyer

Midway International
P.O. Box 777   K-4550 Euroville   Yourland

Mr Bruce Dundee
Ultimate Pty
4130 Pacific Drive
Brisbane
Australia   April 10, 1999

Dear Bruce,

Michael, who's on holiday this week, has asked me to write to warn you that your order UP/901 for 10 OP 232s is going to be delayed. We are very sorry about this but there is not much we can do. The manufacturers have had some difficulties with unreliable CPUs but they have solved these problems by finding a supplier in the USA. We now plan to ship to you on 2 May by airfreight – but if we do manage to get our delivery earlier, we will put them straight on the plane to you.

I have also been asked to mention that although more reliable CPUs are being used (68020s instead of 68000s), the processing speed is reduced from 12 MHz to just under 10 MHz. I don't think this will affect your use of the units, though. We are asking the manufacturer to reduce the price and if they agree to do this, we will pass this saving on to you in full.

One more thing: could you give us a few comments on the OP 424 series? We would like to know your reactions to the price, packaging and design of this product. If you have had any problems with reliability, could you let us know about that too, please?

Thanks for your patience. We will send you a fax as soon as the OP 232s are ready to ship.

Best wishes to Sheila.

Yours,
Your name
for Michael Meyer

15.6 The Peterborough Effect – 1   *Reading*

1 a 2 c 3 b 4 c 5 b 6 c 7 a 8 c 9 c 10 b

15.7 The Peterborough Effect – 2   *Reading*

1 b 2 a 3 b 4 a 5 b 6 c 7 c

15.8 Prepositions revision

1	of	about	6	from	at
2	on	from/for	7	With (GB) / In (US)	to
3	of	in	8	on	in
4	in	of	9	with	for
5	on	of	10	on	on

15.9 Franchising   *Listening*

Ⓑ The missing words are underlined:

1 an <u>established</u> product or service and a well-known <u>brand</u> image.
2 an <u>operating</u> manual, showing how the business should be set up and how it must be run.
3 help, advice and training in <u>setting up</u> the business.
4 continuing advice, training and support during the <u>life</u> of the franchise.
5 the <u>equipment</u> that's required to set up and operate the business.
6 <u>stock</u> of the product, which he will be able to <u>obtain</u> cheaply in <u>bulk</u>. This may result in savings or, depending on the franchisor's mark-up, <u>commit</u> the franchisee to buying at <u>above</u> the market price.
7 local, national and even international <u>advertising</u>.

Ⓒ

1 c   2 b   3 c   4 b   5 a   6 b   7 c   8 b   9 b   10 a

Transcript

Speaker: Now I'll assume you all know what a franchise is. Yes? So let's have a look at the roles of the franchisor and the franchisee. In most cases the franchisor usually supplies seven things.

Firstly, an established product or service and a well-known brand image. And then he'll supply an operating manual, showing how the business should be set up and run. He'll also supply help, advice and training in setting up the business. He'll normally give continuing advice and training during the life of the franchise. And then he'll normally supply all the equipment that's required to set up the business. Then he'll continue to supply a stock of the product, which he'll be able to obtain cheaply in bulk. This may result in savings, or depending on the franchisor's mark-up, commit the franchisee to buying at above market price. And lastly, he'll be responsible for local, national and even international advertising.

Questioner: Sorry to interrupt, but I think it's important to emphasize that the on-going support you mention may vary a lot from franchise to franchise. The brand image of the product and the level of help you get at start-up are visible. But what is likely to happen after, say, twelve months of operating the franchise is much harder to foresee. For example, if things go wrong and your profits are low, you need to know what kind of help you're likely to get – do the franchisor's advisers or trouble-shooters visit regularly? Do they have a mobile back-up team to take over in an emergency? I think it's important to be clear about things like that. Are there any other things like that you need be beware of?

Speaker: Oh, yes. Yes, I agree with you about the importance of this. Yes, there are many other aspects of continuing support.

You need to know if there will continue to be refresher courses to retrain staff – and if there are, will these courses be good and how much will they cost? You'll also want to know if the franchisor is devoting part of his profits to on-going research and development of the product. And you also want to be sure that, if he's charging you a levy for advertising, that this money's actually being spent on advertising. That kind of thing. But let's discuss this later on.

Questioner: Thank you. Yes.

Speaker: Now, if we look briefly at the other side of the operation: what the franchisee brings to the business. The first thing he brings – I'll call the person he, though of course it may well be a she! The first thing he brings is capital: he has to pay a capital sum to buy the franchise for a particular territory: for a big hamburger franchise this could be as much as half a million pounds. Of this, normally, 30% would be the franchisee's own capital, and 70% from a bank. Banks look very favourably on franchises.

He also has to pay a monthly fee to the franchisor, this is usually based on percentage of sales – not profits. There may also be an advertising levy.

He also has various commitments under the terms of his contract, some of which have a good side and a bad side. For instance, he's committed to following the franchisor's methods. Also he can't sell the franchise without the franchisor's agreement. You also know that he's obliged to show the franchisor all his documents and sales figures and he is also committed . . .

Acknowledgements

The authors and publishers are grateful to the authors, publishers and others who have given permission for the use of copyright material identified in the text. In the cases where it has not been possible to identify the source of material used the publishers would welcome information from copyright owners.

p. 7 © *The Economist* (24.11.90);   p. 10 © *The Economist* (24.11.90);   p. 28 'Clear that desk' by Susan Pape from *InterCity Magazine* December 1991/January 1992, reproduced by permission of *InterCity Magazine*;   p. 35 © *The Economist* (7.3.92);   p. 48 reproduced by permission of the Co-operative Bank;   p. 54 © *The Economist* (20.6.92);   p. 57 © *The Economist* (20.6.92);   p. 71 photos by Julien Vonier/Swatch © Swatch;   p. 72 *The Guardian* for the article by Ben Laurance (12.6.93);   p. 80 © *The Independent* for the article by Cary Cooper (10.6.90);   p. 87 © *The Economist* (11.8.90);   p. 93 © *The Economist* (11.8.90); p. 102 adapted from *Negotiate in French and English* by Pamela Sheppard and Bénédicte Lapeyre, Nicholas Brealey Publishing Ltd, London, 1993;   p. 107 David and Rosemary Brown for the crossword puzzle;   p. 112 Commission for the New Towns.

Design and DTP by Newton Harris